HOW TO GET INTO THE
ENTERTAINMENT
BUSINESS

Behind-the-Scenes Jobs That Pay
$100,000
or More a Year!

RON TEPPER

JOHN WILEY & SONS, INC.

New York • Chichester • Weinheim • Brisbane • Singapore • Toronto

This book is printed on acid-free paper. ∞

Published by John Wiley & Sons, Inc.
Published simultaneously in Canada.

This publication is designed to provide accurate and authoritative information in
regard to the subject matter covered. It is sold with the understanding that the
publisher is not engaged in rendering professional services. If professional advice
or other expert assistance is required, the services of a competent professional
person should be sought.

Library of Congress Cataloging-in-Publication Data:

Tepper, Ron, 1937–
        How to get into the entertainment business : behind-the-scenes
jobs that pay $100,000 or more a year! / Ron Tepper.
            p.   cm.
        Includes index.
        ISBN 0-471-32620-8 (pbk : alk. paper)
        1. Performing arts—Vocational guidance—United States.
        I. Title.
        PN1580.T36   1999
        791'.023'73—dc21   98-51507

Printed in the United States of America.

10 9 8 7 6 5 4 3 2 1

Acknowledgments

This book would not have been possible without the assistance of Jeff Keowns and Bob Levinson, who helped set up many of the interviews with the talented, award-winning behind-the-scenes entertainment personalities who are featured throughout this book. Nor would it have been possible without the backing and assistance of Michael Hamilton of John Wiley & Sons, Inc.

Contents

CHAPTER TWO
The First Breaks—How to Find Them   /   39

CHAPTER FIVE

More Opportunities, Plus the Pitfalls, Money, and Future / 135

<u>CHAPTER SIX</u>
Inside Tips and a Look Behind the Scenes / 167

Index / 209

Introduction

While most of the country (and world) worries about the stock market and the impact of overseas purchases on our well-being, there is one segment of our economy that continues to thrive—and will continue to do so—regardless of what happens in Japan, England, or South America.

That segment is entertainment. Late last year USA Networks, Inc. Chairman Barry Diller told his executives "not to lose sleep" over the jittery stock market and the threat of a worldwide recession brought on by the financial crisis in Russia, Asia, and Latin America. In a page one story in The Los Angeles Times, Diller said at a meeting of his top executives that USA's "television, concert ticketing, and Internet businesses are virtually recession-proof because consumers take refuge in entertainment during tough times."

Diller is right. Historically, families continue to go to movies, rent them, and buy CDs. Certainly, they may cut down on the amount of their entertainment budget, but they still buy. "Hollywood," says Diller, "feels less 'pain because it peddles inexpensive serums for escape rather than big ticket discretionary items (i.e., cars, refrigerators).'" And as Diller would say, "There is no business like show business" and no industry that has higher unemployment—or more opportunity.

How to Get into the Entertainment Business is a book about the tremendous opportunities in the entertainment industry. It is a book that focuses on more than 30 high-paying, behind-the-scenes (and behind the camera) positions that are available . . . today!

It is not a theoretical book, rather it is a practical guide that shows you, step-by-step how others broke into the business and became successful. Throughout, you'll find the thoughts and advice from two dozen of the most successful entertainment professionals in the business. They tell you what they decided, and how they climbed the ladder. They outline each step they took, the opportunities, pitfalls, and they show you exactly how you can duplicate their success.

One of the amazing things about these 25 special professionals, is that few, if any, had specialized training. They had talent, creativity, and perseverance, the trio of requirements that will land more jobs for someone in entertainment than all the degrees available.

Entertainment is not about degrees, it's about ability and fortitude. If you want to become an award-winning producer, cameraman, announcer, or whatever—you can. It's a longshot business, but it is difficult only because most people who enter it tackle it the traditional way, that is, they send a resume or make a telephone call and wait.

That's not the way it is done. In this book you'll find some remarkable success stories; most of the time these people succeeded because they followed a few, simple basic rules. For instance, they worked hard. But, hard does not mean the number of hours you put in a job. Rather, it refers to the effort you put out in the amount of time you are on the job.

Perhaps Jeff Olds, a Generation Xer, who entered the industry at the lowest level and through creativity, talent, and an unparalleled work effort, put it best: "When I first got in the business, I was determined to do the best I could at whatever they asked me to do. If my job was making coffee, I resolved to be the best coffee maker they ever had. I was convinced that if I did everything well, to the best of my ability, and if I put forth a maximum effort, they would remember me."

They did, and it wasn't long before Olds became part-owner of one of the hottest new shows on the air. How Olds did it is detailed in this book. The steps he (and others) took not only to get their first entertainment jobs, but to climb the ladder, are outlined so that anyone can follow and emulate their successes.

This book is about how someone who truly wants to enter this exciting, dynamic business can do so. In it, you'll find a wealth of potential entertainment occupations ranging from directors, producers, executive producers, promotion managers, and talent coordinators, to voice-over announcers, cartoonists, screenplay writers, segment producers, TV editors, news cameramen, website producers, animators, and costume designers.

Most important, you'll be able to follow these people from their entry-level positions to the top of their field. None say it was easy, but all say it was possible—and it still is. Those included are:

- *Chuck Bowman*, Emmy-award winning television producer and director, who started out as a disk jockey in a small, midwestern town and went from associate producer on Robert Conrad's *Baa Baa Blacksheep*, to director for series such as the *Incredible Hulk* and V. Along the way, he won a Golden Mike award (the symbol of excellence in broadcasting) for news coverage. Chuck reveals the path he took to success, the roadblocks, and how he overcame them. He also discusses his unusual "indoctrination" into the business—as an usher in a movie theater.

- *Richard Alvarez*, an 18-year veteran TV photojournalist, who turned editor for the Los Angeles' CBS affiliate, and won an Emmy for one of the most talked-about exposés ever to air on L.A. television—the restaurant story, a lengthy, in-depth report in which Alvarez and his fellow newspeople unveiled the seamier (unhealthy) sides of L.A. bistros. The series was such a hit, that legislators later rated every restaurant in the city and had rating sheets displayed in every window.

- *Craig Miller* practically invented the term *niche marketing* (in motion pictures)—a promotion effort designed to publicize a film to a select segment of the market. Miller handled one of the biggest hits ever, *Star Wars*, and designed and conducted the campaign that would help George Lucas reach every sci-fi buff in the country. Today, Miller has become one of the top producers of animated cartoon series, and has worked on a variety of shows including (as a writer) *Real Ghostbusters* and *Babylon 5*. But, it is as a series developer that Miller shines. His series, *Pocket Dragon Adventures* is on the BKN Kids network and airs on 85 percent of the country. Miller talks about a variety of steps he took in climbing the ladder, especially networking and how to use contacts.

- *Robert Brown*, a legendary actor who starred in the television version of *Seven Brides for Seven Brothers* appeared to be headed for a lifelong career in acting (he was doing 10 to 20 plays a year, including Shakespeare), until the voice-over bug struck and he became one of Hollywood's most in-demand voices. You'll recognize him on everything from Porsche to the voice of Iams' dog food. What makes a good voice-over announcer and, more important, how do you break into the business? What characteristics do voice-over personalities and actors share? Brown answers all the questions, including the tough ones on how he climbed to the top.

- *Michelle Baxter*, who started as a singer in a band and worked her way "up" to an internship at a television station in New England, is typical of the budding entertainment hopefuls who work hard, long hours for (at first) little money. Eventually, Michelle—who is still in her 20s—made it as a segment producer on MTV.

- *Andy Epstein*, dual Emmy Award winner, went through a variety of positions before he finally landed one as a producer who handled everything from *Hard Copy* (in the field) to *Entertainment Tonight* and finally as one of the top investigative producers/reporters in the nation. Today, he produces one of the most competitive news segments (for CBS) in Los Angeles. He offers sound advice and steps to take for budding reporters, producers, editors, and photojournalists.

- *Bob Schulenberg* is noted for producing *Eating Raoul*, the classic, 1981 film that swept the Los Angeles and New York film festivals, and became the forerunner for Jim Carrey's *The Truman Show*. Along the way, Schulenberg, one of the most talented animators in the business, has had his work seen on stage, screen, and in some of the most prestigious magazines in the country. His mastery of classic animation is a tale filled with advice and critical lessons about breaking into the business.

- *Les Rose*, a freewheeling, five-time Emmy award winner, has been a staff photojournalist for more than a dozen years, and his rise is a lesson in perseverance as well as what it takes to make it in entertainment. Rose sent 186 resumes out to try and land his first major job, but what got him the job was a daring gesture he decided to try; a gesture that landed him a job and a career, 3,000 miles from home.

- *Jerad Grimes* is one of the newcomers to the business, but he's also a perfect example of how someone can completely switch careers and still make it. Grimes, who has produced segments for the *Dating Game*, and is waiting for the next step—executive producer—gave up a promising law career in Arizona and threw everything away for a shot at entertainment and Hollywood, where he started as a production assistant in a job that he held for one day!

- *Jeff Olds* has a success story that sounds like fiction. A University of Colorado graduate, heading for a career in the diplomatic corps, he was bitten by the entertainment industry bug when he worked—part time—on college campus to promote movies. That experience was all it took. Olds gave up politics and headed for California, where he worked as a waiter in a restaurant, but ultimately found the road to success and today owns (and is executive producer) of one of the hottest shows around, *Biorhythm*, the musical biography series that has helped make MTV one of the most popular music channels in the business.

- *Erick Finke*, the son of a prominent patent attorney, found a way to get into the business by working as an intern on a local cable access channel. That experience not only got him behind the camera, but taught him about the type of things that work, what keeps an audience's attention, and how you put together award-winning websites on the Internet.

- *Peter Lefcourt*, one of the most talented television and screenwriters in entertainment, remembers selling his first story (to television) for $2,500 and then having the rug pulled out when the executives changed and no one wanted his story. An Emmy-award winner (*Cagney & Lacey*), he did everything from teaching to driving a cab before he found success.

- *Erica Huggins*, an executive producer, producer, and former film editor had a meteoric rise in the industry. From an interest in anthropology, she has built one of the most promising careers in the industry and is executive producer on the recent Robin Williams' film, *What Dreams May Come*.

- *Jay Lowy*, former president of the National Association of Recording Arts and Sciences (NARAS) and a publisher's representative/song plugger revolutionized the business with the way he handled the Motown Records' catalog. His track record insofar as getting songs published is second to none. He tells how he did it and the surprising things he sees in the future of music and song publishing.

- *Paul Addis* is a personal manager who has brought a new way of doing things to the business. He shows how much more money can be made if personal managers change their methods slightly and incorporate some innovative marketing techniques into their daily operation.

- *Nancy McCook*, a long-time, enormously successful casting director, got started on the switchboard and learned the trade. She talks about the way to break into the business, the changes that are going on, and why many agents are becoming casting directors instead of the other way around.

- *Dean Rick Jewell* of the University of Southern California film school gives his assessment of the industry today, where it has been, and the surprising directions it may be going and how it will impact those behind-the-scenes.

- *Tony Selznick*, choreographer/dancer agent, explains how the business has changed, the unusual thing that has happened to choreography, and how to break into the agency business with one simple technique that is just beginning to spread across the industry.

- *Tom Sanders* is hard to describe—a "free-fall cinematographer" who is part stuntman part cameraman, does something only a few others in the entire industry have attempted: shooting video, film, and stills using three cameras as he jumps out of airplanes. Sanders made his mark as the photojournalist who followed former President George Bush and photographed the chief executive as he celebrated his birthday by parachuting out of an airplane.

- *Don Graham*, the man responsible for the emergence of A&M Records, the breaking of Peter, Paul, & Mary as a top act, and the country's leading record promoter, explains how things are today in the promotion business, the important changes that are going on, and the ease with which someone can break into the business.

- *Brick Price*, the most unique special effects man in the country, uses miniatures as well as full-size props in making films and his approach has become the talk of the industry. He won an Oscar for the role he played in the special effects in *The Abyss*.

- *Tisha Fein*, the daughter of renowned personal manager Irving Fein, has become the most celebrated talent coordinator in the country. She handles talent for every variety and awards show imaginable and provides some insight into how others can emulate her phenomenal success and track records. She is a winner of multiple awards.

- *Bill Royce*, writer, producer, talent coordinator—Emmy Award winner—and a veteran contributor to *Good Morning, America* and *The Today Show*. Royce is noted as co-producer of the phenomenonally successful *The Tonight Show with Jay Leno*, and he broke into the business when he was barely in his twenties. His ability and techniques on the telephone enabled him to land positions with some of the most prestigious television shows in the country.

CHAPTER ONE

Background and Needed Characteristics

W hat does it take to make it into the entertainment business? It only takes persistence, perseverance, commitment, chutzpah (daring), and a lot of luck. Then add talent and creativity. It takes all that and more, but despite these obstacles, people do it every day.

Although we seldom think about it, those in entertainment are among the most entrepreneurial individuals in the country. They are usually self-employed, self-starters. They may not have retail storefronts, but they are dependent on their own efforts and relationships for their next paycheck. Entertainment is glamorous, but it is also a tough business. Many of those in this business generate income in the six- and seven-figure range, but they work hard, long hours and their efforts can be deflated by one bad review, which can close a production, destroy box office revenues, cause the cancellation of a television production or lose someone a radio talk show or commercial.

College Not the Way In

This is not a business where a college education earns you a shot at a job. In fact, young, fast-rising Erica Huggins, executive producer of Robin Williams' *What Dreams May Come*, will tell you that college will not prepare someone for the business. Only the business can. "But," says Bill Royce, co-producer of the *The Tonight Show with Jay Leno*, "don't discard one thing college will teach you—responsibility. In entertainment, when you get a job, no one shows you how to do it. You have to do it yourself; be responsible. Responsibility is one of the most important characteristics in this business."

This is not a business, however, that you get into by answering an ad in the classifieds for a management trainee, either. The most likely way someone makes it—"on-the-job training." Indoctrination and training usually starts in the mailroom, where prospective behind-the-scenes entertainment industry employees cart packages and deliver messages, or as a runner (better known as a "gopher") where they fetch this and that, walk dogs for well-known performers or high paid emcees, and do any job—odd or not—that has to be done.

Entertainment is glamorous—when you get to be one of the behind-the-camera stars, but until then it is hard work, long hours, weekend duty, and minimum wage. In fact, many have made less than a fast-food worker at McDonald's while they climbed the ladder. Why don't more people make it? Primarily because not enough of the entertainment hopefuls who search for behind-the-scenes opportunities are willing to do menial work to make their dreams come true. The common thread shared by all who were interviewed was that they were willing to do any kind of work in pursuit of their aspirations, and they did it willingly because of their zest, zeal, drive, and strong personality characteristics.

What kind of characteristics? Take Tom Sanders, a daring photojournalist, who is half stuntman, half photographer. Sanders specializes in parachuting out of airplanes with two or three cameras strapped to his helmet. He's one of only four free-fall cinematographers in the country who are talented enough (and crazy enough, some would say) to leap out of an airplane and shoot video, film, and stills at the same time. To top it off, Sanders will tell you that the only reason he jumped in the first place was because he was scared.

Today, Sanders, whom many remember as the stuntman/photographer who followed former President George Bush into the wide open air spaces as he jumped out of an airplane to celebrate his seventy-second birthday, finds it hard to believe that his greatest fear (before he started jumping) was heights.

"I couldn't stand them," he recalls, "so I took a class—call it positive thinking—where the ultimate test and technique that was used for building your confidence was tackling your worst fear head-on. For me that was parachuting out of an airplane. When the instructor told me I would have to do it, I thought he was crazy . . . but I did it and at the same time discovered a new career and an incredible business."

Sanders, who is noted for his unique aerial photography (he carries a video, film, and still camera), never took a class in the subject, so how did he learn photography? How did he become one of the premiere stuntmen/cinematographers in the business?

"Believe it or not, when I got my first camera, I read the instructions carefully . . . and over and over again. The trouble with most people is they just peruse directions, especially when it comes to cameras. It's only natural, especially with today's technology, that most of us think all we have to do is point and shoot. All I did was follow the directions, which is what most people do not do. Good pictures are made that way, and you will never make a career out of photography if you don't follow the directions."

The camera, he says, is like anything else. If you do not study and work at it you will never be any good. "It takes commitment, like everything else in this business."

Commitment is vital in every industry, especially entertainment. Few breaking into an industry hear as many "no's" as those who are trying to create a behind-the-scenes show business career. You need a thick ego and a driving personality.

How Emmy Award Winner Did It

Les Rose has it. Who else would send "186 resumes out trying to get a job in television news. I used to put my rejection letters on my bedroom wall in my one-room apartment. It was the most unusual and colorful wall in the building," laughs Rose, a five-time Emmy award-winning photojournalist and television cameraman.

Rose, like Sanders, has daring, too. Once, while working in Florida, he discovered there was a job opening in Los Angeles with the CBS affiliate. He wanted desperately to come to Los Angeles, but knew his chances were minimal. Many have faced similar situations, and they may have given up. Not Rose.

"I knew that whatever news director did the hiring was going to first look locally. In a market like Los Angeles, which is loaded with talent, there is no need to mess with someone 3,000 miles away, like I was." But, that did not discourage Rose. Without blinking, he sent a tape which showed his photographic ability through some of the stories he had covered in Florida. Then he called, and he still remembers the conversation.

"I was competing against every local talented photographer in L.A. I said one thing to the hiring manager—'if I fly 3,000 miles to see you, will you give me five minutes?' He probably thought I was crazy, but he said yes—and I landed the job."

Outrageous? Daring? Of course, "but to make it in this business you have to do the unusual," says the outspoken, talented photographer. "Make sure they remember you."

Not many could forget Rose. Born in Nebraska and raised in Florida, he appeared to be heading for a career in medicine until "organic chemistry got me. So I switched. I tried a little of everything, including history and then mass communications." His first encounter with entertainment was typical of many of those who have made it—"I earned money through college by being a disk jockey. It may sound like a cliché, but I took to it like a duck to water. I loved the excitement."

Rose did not remain a disk jockey for long before he landed what has become one of the career building blocks in entertainment—an internship. "I landed one and believe me that is the most valuable thing you can do if you want to get into this business. Become an intern. The hours are crummy, the pay is lousy, but you learn the business."

THE IDEAL STARTING OPPORTUNITY

Rose, who was to garner five Emmy's at a major television station, landed his internship at a radio station. "It wasn't a giant outlet," he says smiling. "It was a small, on-campus station, but starting out like that is ideal. You do everything. Contrast that with a major, network affiliate where I might have been pigeon-holed and never had the benefit of learning everything. I might have been stuck as a messenger running copy all day."

Because it was small, Rose did everything, from writing to editing copy. "Take it from me, when you get your first position, small can be beautiful. You don't want a large corporate setup where you are stuck in one job. Look at every position as an opportunity. I've seen many in the field go from a runner to a producer, simply because they jumped on the opportunity. If you're not an opportunist, this business is not for you."

Emmy Award winner Bill Royce knows about opportunity. He was a criminology major at the University of California (Berkeley), but he always harbored a desire to make entertainment a career. Despite his major, he dabbled in entertainment and wrote film reviews for the college newspaper. During a visit to the nearby San Francisco Film Festival, he met gossip columnist/television personality Rona Barrett. Even today—20 years later—he remembers it well.

"I was star struck," he recalls, "just like everyone else. Most of us were afraid to talk to a celebrity when we met one. But I took the opportunity. Despite the qualms, I introduced myself." That introduction eventually led Royce to his first entertainment job—with Rona Barrett.

Andy Epstein and Erica Huggins know about Rona Barrett and taking advantage of opportunities too. Epstein, a dual Emmy award-winning producer, started out doing investigative pieces for the entertainment section of *The Los Angeles Times*. His work was spotted by gossip columnist Barrett, who brought him to *Good Morning, America*, and from there to *Entertainment Tonight*.

"I went from 5,000 piece articles to 30-word stories," he says, "but regardless of what you are doing and for whom, do it the best you can. Take advantage of every opportunity, whether it is as a messenger or director."

Epstein's rise was not easy or quick. He did his share of working in mail rooms and taking on menial jobs, but one of those positions taught him a great deal about consumers, what they are like and what they will buy. Through his father—one of the top local newspaper writers in Los Angeles, Epstein had met Bob Levinson, a public relations' (PR) guru who had guided the careers of some of the industry's best-known talents. Levinson hired Epstein to work in the mailroom, and he began to learn the business.

PR people always try to get their clients and products exposed by the media. They are constantly trying to sell media on doing a story, and being one of them—even for a short time—helped Epstein see how hooks and angles were developed.

"That experience helped me see how PR people created stories and news angles about entertainers that they sold to the media. It helped me learn what people wanted to see, read, and hear. I learned about the gossip, the consumer's fascination with it and entertainment, and later, when I was in the position of trying to find stories for the shows I worked with—*Hard Copy, Entertainment Tonight, Good Morning, America*—I had an advantage. I had already been trained in finding those hooks and angles by Levinson.

Some might say Epstein was just lucky to land the position with Levinson. But Levinson was more than an employer, he was a mentor. That, more than anything, is "what people need if they are going to break into this business," says Erica Huggins, the young Interscope (subsidiary of Polygram) executive producer/producer.

Erica credits two mentors (film editor Janice Hampton and entertainment executive Robert Cort) with her rapid emergence. "They put themselves out there for me. Find someone you can learn from, and by watching and getting 'inside their head' you will learn. None of the positions in entertainment (or film) are clear cut. There are a lot of subtle avenues, and a mentor can help you find your way."

Huggins had little trouble finding hers. From the beginning, the executive—who was initially headed toward a career in anthropology and documentary films—had been interested in "good storytelling, one of the keys to good filmmaking." In college, while majoring in anthropology, she and her partner did a 20-minute film called *The Subject*, a love story. "That's what got me interested in editing" which would turn out to be her first job in Hollywood.

"Even though I did not know a thing about entertainment or Hollywood (her father is a psychologist and her mother is a schoolteacher), "editing our film fascinated me." It may have ended there were it not for a friend, who invited her to Cannon Films. On the strength of her brief film experience, Erica was offered an apprentice editor position at Cannon, where she worked on *Firewalker* with Chuck Norris. That was the beginning.

Although successful entertainment careers involve an element of luck and mentoring, networking—as experienced by Huggins—can be extremely important. There is, in fact, few things more important for anyone in the business, than networking. Regardless of how high someone climbs in the business, they do not make it without other people. It is a business built on relationships.

"Relationships are key," says multi-award winning commercial announcer Casey Kasem. Kasem, who is best known as the voice of *American Top* 40, says "you have to be in the middle of what's happening. That means meeting people." Kasem did. In fact, if it wasn't for a friend who virtually forced him to contact a commercial agent, Casey might still be a disk jockey in the midwest.

Tisha Fein, who has been the talent coordinator on virtually every major awards show on television, agrees with Casey's relationship assessment and adds one other characteristic: "You have to be good with people, and you need a great sense of humor in the business."

Segment producer Michelle Baxter, who started at WWOR in New York and then moved to MTV, says "you have to be a people person. Instinctively know them." Jay Lowy, former president of the National Academy of Recording Arts and Sciences (NARAS) says that throughout the years one thing has not changed—"this is a people business. I know that is an overused term, but in entertainment it is true. It's who you've met and who you know. People remember."

RELATIONSHIPS ARE KING

Tony Selznick, who manages choreographers, nods agreement. "This is a connection business, built on friendships. In this business you find out that your friendship does mean something." That does not mean, of course, that you have to be slapping people on the back, but it does indicate how important it is to meet people wherever someone goes in the business. Relationships are king.

"Learn how to talk on the telephone," says Royce. "Try to make it stand out. If people remember you from the telephone—that is, they remember your personality—you will get in the door. I have a whacko sense of humor that comes across on the telephone. If you have a similar ability, it can be an enormous advantage. People look forward to talking to you."

Personal manager Paul Addis adds one more ability. "You need to be a salesman and understand marketing in my end of the business. Creative is one thing, but when you are a deal-maker and negotiating with labels, you need a good business sense. Artists (clients) look to us for that ability."

Unquestionably, one of the major characteristics found in any successful career is networking. It is an overused and abused term, but in entertainment it is a vital component. Most of those in this book can trace their successful moves to the days when they were interns and met someone who later played a key role in their career development. Networking is vital in entertainment for another reason. Unlike the corporate world where executives may spend two, three, or even five years (even in today's rapidly changing business climate), many positions in entertainment are short-lived. Downsizing and rightsizing have taken their toll in the corporate world, but they pale in comparison when you look at a show that debuts and is cancelled after the first two episodes.

How It Differs from Corporate World

Some series may last for 13 weeks or less, a producer can be fired, a director replaced, a storyline completely changed. Whatever the length of a show, series, or so on, there is a unique camaraderie built among those on (or behind) the set/show. It differs from the corporate world, where the fate of one executive usually does not depend upon the fate of another. A CEO can be fired without disturbing the executive vice president or CFO. In entertainment, however, if the executive producer goes because the network or money people are unhappy, there's a good chance the rest of the executives and creative people will go, too. Hence when a producer goes to another show, they tend to reach back and pluck those who were with them. A loyalty has been built and a bond formed.

Still, a person does not move from one show to another unless they have shown talent, skill, creativity, and an endless work ethic. Andy Epstein had it. He was not, however, an overnight success. In the entertainment field, there isn't any such phenomena. Nearly every successful person in the business has gone through difficulties, and if there is one thing they have all learned it is that there is nothing as predictable as the unpredictable nature of the business. Entertainment, like other enterprises, depends on sales (ratings, box office receipts, etc.) but those in it are frequently at the mercy of sponsors and others who want to attract 18 to 34 year olds to their films and productions.

Nancy McCook, a former agent and active casting director, knows the demographic wars well. "It is not just a matter of demographics today," she says. "The teenage girl who has 14 earrings in her ear influences the advertisers and they, in turn, make demands on casting directors. For instance, instead of actors and actresses being sought after (for commercials), real people are in-demand." What are real people? "A slice of life, the people who look like those you see on the street. They are not necessarily handsome or pretty, but they are real. The business is radically different today than it was a few years ago."

"Advertisers are running around asking casting directors and agents for slice-of-life people, and demanding show producers to come up with clones of Beverly Hills 90210. Those behind-the-scenes on entertainment shows, find that the news has to be more sensational in order to pique an audience's interest and capture the ratings."

HOW THE BUSINESS IS CHANGING

With all this happening, the person trying to carve a niche in the business has to closely watch and listen to what's going on.

Nancy does that well. She monitors television nightly, sees every top motion picture, reads the daily newspapers religiously, and listens to radio as well. "The business—like all other enterprises—is changing. Just one example. Years ago, celebrities would not be caught in a commercial. Today, we are besieged by stars who want to be in them. Everyone has discovered there is money in commercials."

To keep pace with the changes, if you are going to enter the business you need to be flexible, a good listener, daring, creative, and risk-oriented. "David Smith" (not his real name) fits the bill. David, who went on to become one of the biggest figures in the motion picture and music industry (eventually partnering with two other prominent figures to form one of Hollywood's biggest studios), almost had his career end before it started. Initially, he began his career as many others—in the mailroom of a well-known theatrical agency.

At the time, the agency had a firm rule: anyone who worked in the mailroom had to have a college degree. David Smith did not, but on his application he fudged. The agency, though, always checked and the human resource department sent a letter to the university that Smith had named as his undergraduate school. All the agency wanted was confirmation that David had, indeed, graduated.

David knew the procedure and was aware it would only be a matter of time before the university filled out the form and notified the agency they had never heard of "David Smith." Every morning, for more than a month, he showed up at the crack of dawn for his mailroom duty. At 6:30 A.M., long before anyone else arrived, David was there. And, for a good reason. Day after day he waited patiently for the postage-paid return envelope that would be sent from the university to the agency's human resource department. Finally it arrived, and David snagged it and dumped it in the round file. Thus, instead of being fired, "David Smith" went on to become one of the industry's most successful figures.

Dishonest? Somewhat. Daring? Yes. Of course. Should "Smith" have gotten away with it? Perhaps not. Still, it is evidence that in entertainment you often find people doing things differently. Take Don Graham, a legendary record promoter who has become one of the top behind-the-scenes record promoters in the country. Graham, who whose career goes back to the 1960s, was responsible for the success of numerous artists ranging from Peter, Paul, and Mary to the Carpenters and most recently Sara Brightman and Andrea Bocelli, the duo that has amazed the world with a multimillion selling opera album (promoted by Graham) called "Romanza."

To get exposure for artists, Graham is noted for doing outrageous, daring things. Typical of his chutzpah and style is what he did to take Peter, Paul, and Mary from anonymity to overnight stardom. Graham, who worked out of San Francisco, was called one day by a label that asked him to meet a new trio—Peter, Paul, and Mary—at the airport. The group was coming in to play the Hungri I, a famous nightspot that had spawned many top artists.

One problem—the Hungri I had not booked the trio. Could Graham get them in? Without hesitation, the young promoter met the trio, took them to the club, and convinced the owner to book them for a three-week run. The pay was so miniscule that the trio could not afford a hotel. So they stayed with Graham.

Graham pondered their fate and the idea hit him. He drove across the Golden Gate to a local college and looked up the council that was responsible for booking talent into the college. Once he found them, he made them an offer they could not refuse. He would provide Peter, Paul, and Mary at no cost to the college for a concert. All they had to do was show up on a designated night (with as many college students as possible) in front of the Hungri I, demanding to hear Peter, Paul, and Mary.

The students—although they had never heard of the trio—agreed. A week later, nearly 600 were shouting outside the club, holding banners up, and demanding to see Peter, Paul, and Mary. The event got so boisterous that the San Francisco police were called to break up the "riot." When the police showed, Graham was there with a photographer who took pictures of the action.

The next day, Graham visited the city's top columnist, Herb Caen. Graham told him the story, and Caen roared with laughter—and ran the pictures along with a story saying how great the new trio was and that no one should miss this engagement. Few did, and within weeks Peter, Paul, and Mary were not only the toast of San Francisco, but their record was sweeping across the country.

"This business," says Graham, "does not require a great deal of intelligence. You need enthusiasm, genuine enthusiasm, and in my end of the business, a record that is good. If you have those ingredients, you can make a career out of record promotion."

THE BREAKS

Breaks are a key part of anyone's career, and everyone in this book has had their share of them—as well as their ups and down. But, for everyone, the doubts, and frustrations were worth it. Some gave up promising careers for an internship, part-time position, or temporary post.

No other industry has as many people who love what they are doing as much as this one. What other explanation is there for an attorney who gave up a burgeoning law career to work for minimum wage at a TV station?

Where else would you find a promising young communications graduate from a prestigious Ivy League school, tossing it all aside to work as an intern for $8 a day in a local station?

Or, for that matter, what other industry has writers working as cab drivers, producers toiling as teachers, and budding creative directors working in fast-food restaurants for minimum wage? And, in what other occupation are you considered "senior" if you last 26 weeks on a job, or change companies three or four times a year?

That's entertainment, a business that has an unemployment rate of more than 90 percent but beckons to people throughout the country (and world) because of the excitement, variety—and big bucks . . . if you make it. And, that's one of the truly fascinating things about entertainment. It may be a long shot, but with the right approach and dedicated work ethic you can make it.

Interestingly, none of those in this book ever thought once they would miss. Most went from (below) minimum wage to awards, triumphs, and six-figure incomes. They are enthusiastic about their trade, and will tell you the opportunity is there—for anyone. One of the keys: Never worry about money.

"If you get hung up in the dollar and cents thing, you will never make it," says multi-award winning animator, producer, and illustrator Bob Schulenberg. In fact, there's no sense in dwelling on money if you are trying to break into the business. The average fast food employee makes more, but the person who sets their sights on entertainment never thinks about how much they should be paid. This is a business where performance is rewarded, and handsomely. If you make it. And, you can.

WHAT EMMY-AWARD WINNER BELIEVES

Peter Lefcourt, screenwriter, is evidence of that. Lefcourt, who won an Emmy for *Cagney & Lacey*, admittedly was an idealist when he was young. He spent two years in the Peace Corps and wanted to get into the foreign service. He even joined the United States Information Agency (USIA) but switched directions when he discovered they "were too uptight in government. They fired me."

Why were things so stringent? Lefcourt laughs when he thinks back. "The State Department was convinced there was a communist plot in Togo. My job was to read the Togo newspapers every day and try and ferret out the anti-American plots." From there, Lefcourt did everything. He taught school, drove a cab, wrote adult fiction for $50 a story, and even moved to Quebec to become a chess hustler for $5 a night. Why Quebec? "I could not afford Paris, so I chose the closest French-speaking city," he explains smiling.

Lefcourt's moves and adventures illustrate one other characteristic of those in the business—they are free spirits. Usually, not held down by roots or worried about how they are going to earn their next dollar. They move where the urge takes them, and rarely worry about where their next meal is coming from. That does not mean someone who wants to get in the business has to be a free spirit or a wanderer, but it does indicate that in order to make it in the business the "average" entertainment behind-the-scenes worker does not think the same as the average worker. Perhaps it is that carefree nature that also allows them to be more creative—a definite requirement and characteristic of all who made it.

Graham is the epitome of someone in the business who has never worried, especially when it comes to money. In his early days as a record promoter, he seldom thought about money. He had just been discharged from the military, and he had saved a significant amount after spending his entire enlistment on a ship that was an icebreaker near the North Pole. "There wasn't any place to spend money."

When he returned from the service, he got into the business and worked for a wage that was barely over minimum, but he did not care. He loved the business. Months later, he was astounded when another employer came to him and offered him a job—at four times the salary he was making. To this day, Graham does not worry about money. He knows with his expertise, there will always be someone who wants his skills.

To shirk those financial fears takes a special kind of person. Lefcourt is an excellent example of that type of individual. After his chess hustling days were over, he got a call from Frank Price, head of Universal Television, asking him if he wanted to come to Hollywood. Price wanted the young writer to put together a screenplay for a television motion picture, and he sent Lefcourt a first-class airline ticket and $2,500.

"I had never seen that much money before," he says, "and it was something different for someone who had been working for $50 a story. I came to California, took an apartment in the Marina (Marina del Rey), and then with the last of the money, made a down payment on a Porsche. I went back to Vermont to clean out my apartment and move to California."

Then, it happened. He received a telephone call telling him the project was dead. Apparently, there were new moguls in charge of the studio and Lefcourt's project was expendable. Whereas, that kind of break would have discouraged most, it encouraged Lefcourt. He wrote a few more short stories, put a bankroll together, purchased a used VW, and with a "few bucks in my pocket, I drove across country to the Promised Land." As we'll see in later chapters, what awaited Lefcourt was not the most promising opportunity.

WHERE POLITICS PLAY A HAND

Politics? Like any other business, entertainment has it. Rose illustrates how it works. He had struggled for months to find a good position in television news, and finally the offer came. A great salary with a first-class station in St. Louis. He packed his Floridian roots and headed to Missouri. One of the first things he had to do was join the Union. He did, and a week later the union struck the station and Rose was walking a picket line. By the second week, he was struggling with his sign through 30 inches of snow. It didn't take Rose long to figure he would be better off (and a lot warmer) in Florida.

Graham has seen similar things. He may have a "hot" record, one that is a sure hit, and he has to deal with two or three major stations in the same market. They listen, and each asks the same question—"Do I get this exclusively?" Obviously, it is physically impossible to give all three an exclusive. But, if Graham can't, he may lose airplay on one, two, or even all three. What do you do? After years in the business, Graham has it figured.

Part of being a successful politician is being an equally adept compromiser. The ability to bring sides together is an art that most successful people in the industry possess. Even when you make it there is usually compromise involved because you are dealing with other creative people who have egos and opinions.

Jeff Olds knows that. Olds, a born salesman—as well as a promotion manager, executive producer, talent coordinator and associate producer—created one of MTV's hottest shows, *Biorhythm*, but not before he learned some harsh lessons about compromise. Olds, who was considered one of the rising young programming and creative stars in the business, was once brought in by Columbia to create a new concept for the *Dating Game*. Olds did. Within three months it was the studio's highest rated syndication show—and then Olds made a mistake. The studio executives wanted him to do something different with the show. He refused and was fired.

THE LESSON IN BEING FIRED

"It was the best thing that ever happened to me. I thought I knew everything, and that I controlled the entire situation. You don't. Sometimes your star rises too quickly, and it can kill you. Your ego is something that can easily get in the way, especially in this business."

What many find is that when they become successful those who were once willing and able to offer sound advice no longer do so. Instead, many of the highly successful industry figures (both in front and behind the camera) are surrounded by "yes" men and women. People who know something is wrong, but do not express their opinion because they do not want to fall out of favor (and perhaps lose a job).

Invariably, those who retain success in the business retain their objectivity. They do not have to rely solely on others for opinions. "What everyone also has to realize in this business," says Olds, "is that ideas and creativity count, but money counts more. Especially the people with money. It's the same in any business. You may be the creative force, but those with the money are paying for the concept and taking the risk. I never forgot that. It was a tough lesson, but worth it. It taught me a number of things aside from who runs the show. Most important, don't let your ego run you. To an extent I did. I was young and brash, and had just been given free reign and created a hot show that was top rated in syndication. I could do no wrong. At least I thought so." In entertainment, as is the case with any business, everyone is replaceable.

Lefcourt has learned something about control and power, too. "Motion pictures for television and movies for theatrical release may appear to be the same thing but they are vastly different insofar as who controls what. When you write a screenplay for motion pictures, the copyright is owned by the studio. You're on the sidelines with little say. The studio does the casting and controls everything. In television, the writer is not only the writer—and the person doing the rewrites—but they are frequently the producer, as well. The writer in television has much more power and influence. No question about that. But, if you are going to write for the big screen you have to compromise."

From Small Town Theater Usher to Director

Chuck Bowman (a multi-award winner with Emmy's and Golden Mikes on his hearth) is a veteran producer and director who is at the pinnacle of his career, but he has not lost sight of the importance of getting along with others in the business. Bowman has analyzed the trade, the people, and what it takes to make it. And, he is well-equipped for the analysis. He has been through it all—from disk jockey and associate producer to producer and finally director. The talented native of Coffeyville, Kansas, has what he describes as a "slightly unorthodox" life story. When he was young, "the one consistency in my life was the movies," he says. "That's where I would go to hide. If I ever got in trouble, I went to see a motion picture. If I needed time to think, I went to the movies."

Thus, it is no wonder that Bowman became—at 16 years of age—an usher in a small movie theater in Kansas City. It was one of the best entertainment learning experiences of his life. Although the wage was minimum, he had the benefit of spending countless hours during breaks and at lunch in the balcony where he would watch films over and over again. Sometimes, as many as 15 or 20 times. The hours were not wasted.

"I learned the art of storytelling. How things went from a beginning to the middle to the end." He traces much of his success back to those early days and it made him realize "how important the art of storytelling is in this business. It was one of the best training mechanisms I ever had."

Storytelling is critical to the success of anything in entertainment, whether it be the six o'clock news or a two-hour drama. Any successful entertainment production invariably has a good story to it, and a characteristic that every successful individual in the business has is their ability to spot a good story and understand what audiences will buy. They do make mistakes. If they did not, there would never be series' cancellations or motion pictures that are flops. The ability to tell and spot a good story is a critical element in anyone's career. Executive producers, producers, directors, writers, editors—they would all flop without that skill.

Storytelling skills and understanding of what a story actually is and how it captivates an audience, is one characteristic that is shared by everyone who is successful in the business. It does not matter whether they are a photojournalist or producer. They know without a story—the intriguing beginning, middle, and end—there is no entertainment. Huggins describes it as "learning the rhythm and listening to the sound." Producing involves a great many things, but the most important is the ability to tell a good story. If that's the case, why do so many films—motion picture and television—end up with poor stories?

"No one," explains Huggins, "doubts that the story, the material, is king. The trouble is that there are so many forces tugging in different directions. They each have a say. The director, the actors, the studio financing the production. They are all inputting and sometimes the story gets screwed up because there isn't a leader."

POSITIONS BUILD ON EACH OTHER

Whether someone starts as an intern, page, messenger or producer, everyone in the industry usually learns more than one specific job or skill. One position builds on another. Most in the industry are generalists, not specialists. Producers can become directors and vice versa. Talent coordinators can become associate producers, while photojournalists can become editors, and agents can become casting specialists.

This characteristic of being able to do more than one job, runs throughout the industry. People are not pigeonholed (i.e., as an accountant typically might be in industry) in one position. Most progress up the ladder. If they are good, they pick up one skill after another.

Regardless of what position they occupy, and how much it pays, those in this book—most in the business—start at the bottom. A good example is Bowman. After high school, he went West and landed a job as a page for NBC. The producing, directing, and executive producer positions were years away.

The page position, however, gave him his first opportunity to learn and move up. Thanks to the page duties, he was able to use NBC's facilities and put together a quality demo tape that he later sent to his hometown radio station in hopes of landing a job.

"They turned me down," recalls Bowman, "but they turned me onto another radio station in Hays, Kansas. It was a college town, and they hired me. I worked every shift, every hour I could get—for minimum wage."

Wages did not matter. It was the opportunity, and it wasn't long before another one presented itself. The owners of the radio station were building a television outlet, and Bowman jumped at the chance to get experience in another media. "I did everything from booth announcer to car commercials. That's what you have to remember in this business, everything is experience and that's worth a million dollars. Sure, you may not be making much more than minimum wage, but the training is incredible. It's like going to school and getting paid for it."

Bowman moved whenever there was an opportunity, and the moves came frequently. From Wichita Falls, Texas, where he trained as a meteorologist, to Oklahoma for sports and weather, to Tulsa for late night movies and weather and a Saturday after-noon show.

Graham knows about moving, too. Although he spent most of his career in San Francisco, the opportunity came one day for a move to Los Angeles, where he would do national promotion for A&M Records. Graham took it. "In this business, it is difficult to stay in one place throughout your career. The opportunities come, and although you never know where they will lead, you have to take a chance."

Obviously, being in the entertainment industry is not con-ducive to a 9-to-5 job and normal home life. Everyone sacrifices, but most don't consider it as that. Entertainment is not just a job or a career, it is a lifestyle. Most in it do not have what is consid-ered "normal weekends." Frequently, they are filming or travel-ing or working on sets or rehearsing.

THE WHO-DO-YOU-KNOW SYNDROME

Ultimately, whether it is motion pictures, radio, television, or music, the question is more "can you do it" rather than "who do you know." Certainly, contacts are of paramount importance, and everyone credits networking with a critical part of their success. But, at the same time, they maintain that politics is minimal. Tal-ent and creativity mean everything. Regardless of who you know, if you cannot perform, you are out. The more skills you learn the greater the chance you have of moving up the ladder.

"Equally important as talent is passion, 'enthusiasm,' and perseverance," says Graham. How else does someone carve a career in an industry that has such high unemployment. Richard Alvarez is one of those with the answer. Born and raised in East Los Angeles, his first job out of school was typical of a budding entertainment industry employee—as a messenger for a local channel. That was more than 20 years ago, and he remembers his duties well. For those who would like to follow in Alvarez's footsteps (an Emmy award winner) he can still describe his initial duties—"I tore wire copy off the machines and took dogs to the groomers for reporters . . . whatever odd jobs there were, I got. And, I did them gladly."

Alvarez, like most of the others, made a choice when he took the messenger job. He had spent four years as a city employee with a solid, stable job in the library. But he gave it all up ("in an instant") to take the messenger's job.

Bit by the bug? Obviously, because Alvarez spent 18 months as a messenger and "I was passed up twice for a position. Finally, one day they gave me a shot and told me I had 90 days to prove myself. Initially, I was one of a two-man camera crew. I carried the recorder, and I wound up toting it for six months. Let me tell you, it's heavy, and although it is lighter today, it is still heavy."

Like Alvarez, most of those in the business remember their initial assignments well. Graham had just been discharged from the service, and he visited a neighbor, who happened to be the West Coast sales manager for a major record label. When Graham walked in, he was astounded. There, in the living room, was a stack of albums from floor to ceiling.

THE FIRST JOB OFFERS

"He asked me if I wanted to go to work for him, and my first question was 'Can I have free albums?' When he said yes, nothing could have kept me away from that job." Nancy McCook was equally as enthused by her first offer. She had been working as a switchboard operator, when a commercial agent offered her a position to train in his company and become an agent.

Rose was a pre-med major "but organic chemistry convinced me I was in the wrong field," he says laughing. I switched to history, but started earning money in the entertainment field to pay my fraternity fees by working as a disk jockey on weekends. I found I loved it."

Olds was bored by the thought of going into the diplomatic corps. "*Entertainment Tonight* looked more interesting than politics." To his parents' horror, he dropped everything and moved to Los Angeles where "I was convinced the entertainment business was the answer. People looked like they had fun."

Schulenberg was going to be a concert pianist and probably would have been were it not for a piano competition he entered. "I lost," he says without a sign of regret, "and decided movies were much more interesting. I had a fixation with the motion picture *Fantasia*, and a skill at painting as well as piano. I decided I wanted to do classic animation. I wasn't sure how I was going to get involved, but I was determined to get into the industry."

Epstein, Rose, Graham, and the others have personality and talent. But, if those two attributes were all it took to make a success, then the entertainment field would have twice the number of people it currently employs. Add one other ingredient to the personality and talent mix—drive. Most successful salesmen have the same ability. "No" does not discourage them. They wanted to make it—desperately—and when things did not go right they came back and tried again. Unlike law, medicine, or other professional careers, those who became successful in entertainment did not plan, step-by-step, a career.

Most of the time, you may not even know where the job is going to take you. Despite the doubts, Olds dumped a legal career for it. His initial introduction to it was not the most glamorous event, but it sold him. During his senior year in college, he landed a job on campus working part-time for Warner Bros. His job—passing out flyers promoting new motion pictures. Obviously, Jeff did not do it in hopes of becoming rich, but he was enamoured with the glamour and excitement of the entertainment business—even if the flyers were 3,000 miles from California.

"You can't think about how much you can make if you are going to get into this business, " he says. "What you need—more than a hunger for dollars—is a commitment."

THERE ARE TWO PLACES YOU MUST GO

When he arrived in California, nothing was planned. "I didn't know what to expect," he recalls, "but I was willing to take the chance. If you want to get into this business, I think you have to have the same attitude. If you are going to make a career out of entertainment, Hollywood is probably one of the two (the other being New York) places you have to go."

Although Olds is relatively young (in his late 20s), his journey has not been an easy one. He has held up applause signs and worked in a Mexican restaurant as a waiter for $6 an hour. It was Ruby Rosa's Mexican Cantina and he remembers it well. He was between jobs and admits, "I was too brash for my own good. I wanted to be a producer, and thought I had built a good track record. I refused to take any job other than the one I wanted. Only trouble, it never came along."

Olds, however, still had to pay the bills. With ego in tow, he went to work for the Mexican Cantina as a waiter. "I turned it into my office," he explains smiling. "I used the telephone in the lobby as my office telephone, and I made calls—when I had to—on my break."

One of those calls was to Disney. It was the one he was waiting to hear. Disney wanted to hire him as executive producer for a new series. But, the $6 an hour waiter held out—"I took a chance . . . I told them I had another offer and would have to weigh both. Was I nervous? Sure. But, one thing you learn in this business is that it is not like working for a corporation. In corporate life, you get used to working in a position for several years, if not more. In the entertainment field, particularly television, many things are short-lived—and you get used to it. Security is not the paramount concern."

Craig Miller was another entertainment hopeful who dropped everything to pursue the industry. A Los Angeles native, Miller was set on becoming a psychologist. He went to UCLA where he earned degrees in child development and social psychology, and had every intention of going into one of those fields. But, Miller had an interest that not only provided a diversion from his studies, but it also brought him in contact with people in the entertainment field.

Lucas Took Note of Sci Fi Ability

From the time he was 13-years-of-age, Miller was hooked on science fiction. In the 1970s, the genre was just starting to take hold and attendance at science fiction conventions and expositions was rarely standing room only. That didn't deter Miller, who became noted for his knowledge and the people who frequented science fiction films.

Miller's knowledge caught the attention of the marketing executives from George Lucas' studio. Lucas had just finished filming *Star Wars*, and, at the time, the studio was looking for every way it could possibly promote the film. Miller's knowledge of the sci fi audiences, who comprised them, and how they could be reached, landed him a job with Lucas—and psychology went out the window.

Three thousand miles away, and a few years before Miller got into the business, Peter Lefcourt was pondering his fate in New York. "I was an idealist," he recalls, "and because of the way I thought I did a number of different things before I finally got into the business. Initially, I never thought about television or motion pictures. I wanted to do something for the nation." Lefcourt was inspired by President John Kennedy's historic "Ask not what your country can do for you, but what you can do for your country." Hence his entry into the Peace Corps and his dream of becoming a foreign service officer.

Then came his big break. A relative who worked in television suggested that he write for television. "I said I would never write for television . . . I was above it!" Lefcourt recalls with a laugh. The relative persisted and set up an interview with a television executive from Universal Studios. A surprised Lefcourt recalls what the executive said. "He told me if I had any movie ideas to send them to him."

While Lefcourt was trying to make a career in Hollywood, Schulenberg—a transplanted Angeleno—was trying to make it in New York. "Getting into this business does not happen overnight. Sometimes you have to shift your goals. For instance, I wanted to do classic animation, or full frame. But there were technological advances that were making classic animation difficult to get into."

Schulenberg eventually made it, but along the way he did everything from working as an art director in a New York advertising agency to working on designs for the "Ice Capades." Schulenberg, who later did the art direction and co-produced *The Secret Cinema*, a 1966 production that is considered the forerunner of Jim Carrey's *Truman Show*, has spent considerable time analyzing the business and what it takes to make it.

"Obviously," he says, "you have to work hard. That's a given, but you also have to be realistic. If there isn't any opportunity, regardless of how good you are there is no place to go." Schulenberg found himself in a number of those situations, yet he always progressed. His secret—adapting. If there was not opportunity down one avenue, he would try something else.

Schulenberg's experience typifies what frequently happens in the entertainment business. You start out working in one position and before you know it you are doing something else. All the successful people in this book displayed the ability to be versatile. No one said "I want to be a director, and I won't do anything else." Entertainment does not work that way. Fledgling people in the business may have their hearts set on becoming an art director, costume designer or set director, but along the way—that is, once they get their first job—they soon find that one job dovetails into another. Unlike the chief financial officer in corporate life who spends their entire career with dollars and cents, the prospective employee in the entertainment field is going to run into a variety of opportunities as they build their career. There is no better example of that than Robert Brown.

Brown's background is one of the most unique. Born in Union, New York, his father was a famous butler who had worked for both Teddy and Franklin Delano Roosevelt, and for years the family lived among the rich and famous. But when circumstances changed, Brown's father had to leave their suburban lifestyle, and they wound up in the Bronx, right in the middle of an Orthodox Jewish neighborhood.

Brown, who has impeccable diction—which is one reason he has become one of the most sought after voice-over announcers in the business—remembers it well. He was the "goy" (non-Jewish) in the neighborhood, and his greatest value (to the neighbors) was on Saturday (or Sabbath) when the Jews could not work or handle money. For help, they turned to Brown who would put the "nickel in the slot for them so they could ride the bus. It was," he recalls, "a wonderful upbringing. It gave me knowledge of two different cultures. I even learned Yiddish."

Brown, who says he was a shy youngster, shares a characteristic that is common with others in the business. "During WWII, I was in the South Pacific on a ship, and every chance I had I watched movies. I loved them, and wanted to be an actor. I'm a dreamer . . . a daydreamer."

When the war ended, Brown still had his dreams, but not enough nerve to get on-stage. "I was really like every kid—they all want to be actors. I probably dreamt and thought about it more than most." Then, one day, the opportunity came. One of Brown's wartime buddies, who had "a great voice and wanted to be in radio had the nerve to audition for a local radio station and he landed a job as an announcer. That gave me the courage. I told my parents—not that I wanted to be an actor, but about my desire to be an announcer. In those days, announcers were accepted, but actors were considered drinkers and women chasers. I could never tell my parents I wanted to be an actor."

THE ROAD FROM LAW TO ENTERTAINMENT

It wasn't long before Brown's deep, expressive voice and looks landed him a job in the entertainment business . . . not as an announcer but as an actor. It was a career that led him to Broadway, motion pictures, television, and, ultimately, to the voice-over studios, where his commercials for Chrysler and Coca-Cola have become classics in the industry.

Long after Brown's voice-over career was in high gear, Jerad Grimes came to Los Angeles to carve a niche in the entertainment field. Grimes, a native of Pace, Arizona, a small town of about 10,000 people, "always wanted to do something to get into the industry." But he did not start out that way. Instead, Grimes, who eventually became an associate producer for MTV, earned a degree in Criminal Justice.

Today, he shakes his head in puzzlement. "I actually worked for the County Attorney for two years. I found there was nothing but bureaucratic bungling and politics. My dreams of being a lawyer went out the window and I decided to head for Hollywood."

From the beginning, Grimes wanted to get into production. He was one of the fortunate few who knew someone, a cousin who worked at Columbia Tri-Star. She helped spread Grimes' resume, and he landed a job as a runner for the day.

"That," recalls Grimes, "is someone who runs for this and that. But, the one thing you have to remember, is whatever your title or what you are running for, do it to the best of your ability. Some people who land a menial job at a studio, don't take it seriously, especially if it is just for one day—like mine was. That's a mistake. People are watching you all the time, and they remember those who do the best jobs. I wound up doing a variety of things that day, everything from helping contestants on the show (*Dating Game*) fill out forms to making coffee and holding up applause signs. Before the day was half over, the big boss came over to me and said the contestants liked me and the crew did, too. Would I be interested in a permanent job . . . was he kidding!"

ONE KEY CHARACTERISTIC

Grimes credits his hiring and rapid rise to another characteristic—a solid work ethic. "I was determined to be one of those people they would remember. Regardless of what they had me do, I would do it better and faster than anyone had ever done it before. If they had me make coffee, it would be the best (and fastest) pot they ever had. I wasn't an 18-year-old kid. I was 24 with a college degree, but I was willing to run and do the grunt work. In this business, if you want the breaks, you have to be willing to start at the bottom and do a great job while you're there. Don't let your ego get in the way. I could have, but I was focused on where I wanted to go."

WEBSITE OVER THE LAW

Erick Finke, a partner in one of the leading Website design firms in the country, was another budding attorney. Instead of coming from Arizona, however, he came from "all over. My father was an attorney, and we lived in places ranging from Phoenix and Germany to Spain. I worked as a waiter, wine steward and even taught classes that helped people prepare for the SAT (Scholastic Aptitude Test).

"But I was always interested in film. I evaluated my abilities and knew I was not a good director, but I was an excellent organizer; someone who could really get things (and equipment) together. I had the ideal skills to become a producer.

"If you are going to get into this business," says Finke, "you have to be open-minded. You have to be willing to do a lot of things . . . things that you would not normally do because of your ego. Paying your dues is more important in this business than any other. Don't expect big money to start. I began as a volunteer, that means no money, with a film company that specialized in political features. It wasn't a Hollywood company, at all. It was located in Massachusetts. For anyone who wants to get into entertainment, you can make inroads in your hometown—if you persevere.

"Every town has a cable station that puts on local programming. Most are just waiting for people to come forward to help. The great thing about many of these local stations is you get to do everything. You might be the producer, director, announcer, or even have a role in the production. The experience is super, and there is nothing like it for background."

How Do You Measure Creativity and Talent?

Rick Jewell, Dean of the University of Southern California School of Cinema, has looked at the progress Erick, Grimes, and many others have made during his 22-year career. "This isn't," he explains, "a business that is an exact science. We had a graduate student here once, a young man who had a 4.0 from Harvard. Yet, he could not make a film to save his soul.

"Creativity and talent are two things you cannot measure on a quiz. Even if you have those attributes, you need—perseverance, personality, and networking ability. Even then, there is no guarantee. The one rule is that there are no rules . . . there is no easy path to success, but there is a path. It is up to the individual to find it, but it can be found."

CHAPTER TWO

The First Breaks—How to Find Them

Sometimes it isn't what you know, but who you know. Take Casey Kasem. The unmistakable and memorable voice of *American Top* 40 and one of the best-known voice-over and commercial specialists in the country, might never have had a voice-over career if it wasn't for a music industry acquaintance who, despite Kasem's reluctance, pushed the talented announcer into an interview with an agent.

Today, voice-over announcers are recognized as skilled, talented pitchmen, but when Kasem first hit Los Angeles, most people looked on them as oddballs. In fact, even though Los Angeles is one of the top commercial centers in the world, there were only two agents in town who even handled voice-over announcers.

Casey, a native of Detroit, found himself in southern California almost by accident. Originally, he had come west to San Francisco, but all the Bay Area people he knew urged him to head south to Los Angeles, where commercial agents and talent were thriving. What they failed to tell him, however, was that there were only two agencies in the entire town.

Still, Casey took the plunge and headed for Los Angeles. "If you want to get anywhere in this business you need an agent." Casey, tracked one down, made an appointment and then, to his surprise, he found himself in the office of a less-than-enthusiastic representative. The agent placed Kasem about 30 feet away and asked him to read.

Perplexed, Casey tried to explain that the agent would never be able to hear him, especially without a microphone. The agent insisted and told Casey not to worry. He would hear him, just fine. So Kasem read, the agent thanked him, said he would be in touch, and quickly ushered the hopeful young voice-over specialist out of his office.

Kasem, of course, never heard from the agent again, and made up his mind he would never see another one. "That experience was enough," he recalls, and he would have bowed out of the business permanently, if it wasn't for a young (18-year-old) record producer named Mike Curb. Curb was in the midst of building one of the most successful recording empires in the country. Kasem had met him almost by accident, and Curb became a fan. He could see potential in Kasem's voice and urged him to see another agent.

"I appreciated the confidence Mike had in me, but I had seen enough voice-over agents," Casey recalls. He told Mike to "forget it" but Curb would not. He pushed Casey and virtually forced him to see an agent named Charles Stern. "Three days after my visit to Stern's office, I was cutting my first commercial, and a couple of days after that I did my first Miller High Life spot."

LUCK, FATE, OR RELATIONSHIP BUSINESS?

Luck? Fate? "This is a relationship business," says Casey, "and in order to get somewhere you have to be in the middle of where things are happening. If it wasn't for Mike Curb I probably would never have ended up in the voice-over business."

Like most, Casey had the ambition and drive and all the required assets, but none of those things guarantee you a job in the business. To break through, it helps to know people—people who know where the openings are; people who can refer you to others who control potential jobs. Unlike other industries, you rarely find entertainment industry openings in the classified section. Occasionally, you see one advertised in the trade papers (i.e., *Daily Variety, Hollywood Reporter, Billboard Magazine*), but for the most part this is a business of connections.

Even college graduates who major in film and/or video run into a stone wall. There are film schools that provide an excellent education, but in the long run, the graduate has the same question as every other job seeker in the industry—where do I go for a job?

"Come May, June, and July, you usually find graduates from film school pounding on the door," says Charles Bowman, "but nobody answers."

THREE THINGS THAT MAKE A DIFFERENCE

Rick Jewell, dean of the University of Southern California film school, agrees with Bowman. "After four years here and a complete film education, there is no guarantee you are going to get a job. That's one of the things we stress at the University. Nobody is going to graduate and walk into a production company and become an editor, producer, or director. There's a long period of indoctrination, working at menial jobs for minimum wage. What counts is perseverance, personality—and contacts. Who do you know? It's always been that way."

Whether you to go film school or not, nearly everyone starts on the same level. That's either as a production assistant, messenger, page, or someone in the mailroom. Brick Price, an award winning (Emmy, Oscar) special effects and miniaturization specialist, who is constantly in-demand (*Apollo 13*, *Deep Impact*, *Star Trek Voyager*), went through the rudimentary steps like everyone else. Now, he points to his son, an 18-year-old who wants to develop a behind-the-scenes career.

"You have to be a jack of all trades to survive, and willing to do everything," says Brick. "My son started as a production as-sistant—a fancy name for a messenger. But, he has stuck to it and learned. One night, they asked him to man a camera. Now he is doing special model building, and he hopes—one day—to be shooting travel documentaries. He very well could end up doing that or any number of things. In this business, you may start out with a specific goal (job) in mind, and before you know it you find yourself doing something else. Once you land a posi-tion, it's up to you where you go. Sometimes, the openings occur when you least expect it."

WHERE TO START

So, where does a hopeful entertainment industry worker go? And what door do they knock on if their specialty is unique? For instance, how does a stuntman get started? The answer? It doesn't really matter where. It can be anywhere, in any phase of the business, with any studio, network, channel, station, or whatever. "Just take it," stresses Bowman, "whatever the oppor-tunity." The key is to first get in the "ballpark. If you don't, you'll never be able to play the game."

For instance, if someone has their goal set on becoming a di-rector, holding out for an internship with a director can be a waste of time. It may never happen. "Don't hold out so long that you hold yourself out of a job and a chance to start," says Bowman.

Getting started in this business is unlike any other. If you want to become a carpenter, one of the logical methods would be to head for the carpenter's union and try and convince some-one that you would make a good apprentice or even a runner. Or head for a construction site and offer to do any type of gopher work available. Or cruise the neighborhoods and look for the local fixit and repair men, and offer to work (and run) for them at a low or minimum wage.

Other occupations can be pinpointed in the same way (electricians, plumbers, etc.). Budding accountants can oftentimes find openings on the bulletin boards of local colleges. The same is true for engineers and computer programmers. Even gardeners and maids can find apprenticeships and places to start.

But, when it comes to entertainment the picture changes. Regardless of what the position the industry hopeful desires, the key step is to get started—anywhere. Work as a runner for a television news department, run errands for a production company, or hold up the applause sign at a Jay Leno type show. Just get your foot in the door.

How to Recognize Opportunities

But, you have to recognize when the door is open. Brick Price, who won an Oscar for his unique special effects, could see the opportunity immediately. He was in the service and was drawing cartoons and illustrations one day when an officer walked in and saw the work. He took Price to see the commanding officer, who put the young animator in the motion picture division. By the time he was discharged, Price had learned all the ins and outs of film animation, and he was ready for the industry. "I was lucky," he says.

Executive producer Erica Huggins does not call herself lucky, but she certainly was in the right place at the right time. She had come to Los Angeles, but not with the intention of making film her career. Her brief fling with movie making occurred in college where she made a 20-minute short for school. That's where she got her first experience as a film editor, one that was to open the doors—to Hollywood. Her fascination, however, was not with Hollywood but with anthropology and documentaries. Then things changed. A friend (the connection) invited her to Cannon Films, introduced her to several executives, told them about her college film experience, and suddenly she was offered the job of assistant editor on *Firewalker* with Chuck Norris. That changed everything.

"I learned how film worked, how to be an assistant editor. The editor I worked with let me cut scenes even though I did not know (aside from the one film we did in college) anything about it. The nice thing about editing is, if you mess it up, it can always be fixed. You still have the cut film."

Erica did not mess anything up. Instead word of her ability spread and New Line Cinema contacted her and offered her a position as assistant editor on *Hair Spray*. She took it and in the process met Janice Hampton and Robert Cort, two film executives who became her mentors. Together, they did two additional motion pictures, but Erica believes the key to her success was Hampton and Cort. "Mentors are marvelous people," she says. "Especially Cort and Hampton." She credits her move up the ladder to both, and says "everyone can use a mentor in this business. You need someone to guide you. I don't just mean to show you how to do the job, because that you learn as you go along with their help." Equally important is understanding the politics of the business—whether we are talking motion pictures or business. "I was lucky; I had Cort and Hampton."

IMPACT OF THE ECONOMY

Even with luck, the entertainment hopeful has a tough road to hoe, but they have advantages. One, for instance, is the economy. In the late 1990s, Asia went into a recession, and while the United States was still in the midst of expansion, the lack of sales in the Far East hurt many companies in a variety of industries. Layoffs were everywhere from Seattle and San Antonio to New England and New Mexico. Every industry eventually felt some of the pullback, and the slowdown was reflected in the price of stocks.

When the economy begins to slow, the number of new small businesses begin to fall, however, network—or multi-level marketing—takes an upswing. Entrepreneurial ventures slow because those with cash hold back, they're leery of what might happen to any new venture. But, multi-level ventures thrive because people worry about their jobs, and in an effort to "hedge" they many opt for multi-level opportunities in hopes that it will offset any loss of income in the event they lose their jobs.

But, what happens to entertainment during these up and down times? The entertainment sector has an odd relationship with the economy. The popular theory is that during recessions and downturns, entertainment does better. When times get tough and money gets tight, consumers may cut back in their purchases of durable goods (i.e., refrigerators, automobiles) but they turn to entertainment for escapism and inexpensive, lighthearted amusement. Comedies flourish. During the Great Depression of the 1930s, there were numerous, off-the-wall, zany motion picture productions that did extremely well. For consumers, entertainment is relatively inexpensive compared to durable and other goods, and for the relief it offers from serious subjects (unemployment, crime) consumers are willing to pay.

Growing Outlets

The entertainment industry worker may have difficulty in finding that first break, but once they do there is an abundance of opportunities. One of the reasons for that opportunity is the growing number of outlets for programming.

Kasem cites the commercial field as an example. "There are more radio, television stations, and other outlets than ever before. That means more opportunity for the voice-over personality."

Background Requirements

Regardless of whether the hopeful entertainment worker is looking at radio, television or print, they enjoy one major advantage over the professional—they do not usually need a degree, nor college training. Imagine the years of study it takes for a CPA, doctor, lawyer, pharmacist, and other professional. Those in entertainment can start with minimal training, and secondly, they can always switch (entertainment) careers if they get bored, tired, or anxious for more variety.

Robert Brown, who is noted for an acting career that includes numerous leading man roles, became a commercial announcer; Richard Alvarez went from photojournalist to investigative news editor; Andy Epstein from a newspaper investigative reporter, to a television entertainment writer, to news director of a network affiliate.

In place of the degree that a doctor, lawyer, accountant, or pharmacist has to have, the entertainment pro needs nothing more than desire; an excellent work ethic; common sense; creativity; a willingness to work long hours, weekends, and nights; some all-important "street-smarts"; and, of course, a love of the business. Sound tough on family life? It is, but if someone can match those requirements they have a shot at the top.

There are some unwritten rules, though. Because of the low (starting) pay and odd hours, those entering the business are usually younger, more flexible, and have less responsibility. It's tough to make it on an intern's salary (if there is one) if you have a wife and three kids (that is, unless your wife is supporting the family). But, if you can throw aside the responsibilities, entertainment beckons.

Jeff Olds is an example of someone who found a way in the business. It's a technique that is easily emulated. Olds, a budding lawyer, got hit by the entertainment bug in his senior year. He was trying to earn spending money and he was hired by Warner Bros. (WB) to help promote WB pictures on campus. "Frankly, I was also bored with the law profession. I wasn't actively seeking something else. I more or less just fell into entertainment."

THE CAMPUS CONNECTION

Olds was introduced to the business by one of the many companies that come on campus, hunt for outgoing, willing college students, and then hire them to promote something—anything from motion pictures to shoes. The jobs are usually posted on bulletin boards or at the student employment center. Interestingly, in many cases you don't have to be a student to get the position, just look young and collegiate. Of course, the students don't get rich, but they get a flavor of the business. Sometimes, the taste is irresistible. It was for Olds.

Working for WB for Olds was more than a job. He tossed aside the law books and fell in love with the entertainment industry the minute he picked up his first flyer (it was promoting a motion picture). What's so enticing about passing out a flyer? Olds found that entertainment had pizzazz, and the legal profession paled in comparison. "I guess it was the excitement," recalls Olds. "I still feel that way about the business. You have to if you are going to get somewhere."

For Olds, the Warner Bros. assignment became more than a job. He ate up the assignment (passing out flyers promoting upcoming new feature film releases) and became one of the studio's best on-campus representatives. "It was my first contact with the business, and I was sold because everyone connected with the project looked like they were having fun."

The money wasn't much but Olds was not in it for a financial killing. Everyone has said it but Olds adds his voice to it— "When you break into this business money is the last thing you should have on your mind. First, concentrate on doing a bang up job. Do the best you can. You only have a short time to impress people, and in this business you only get one chance to make a first impression."

Olds made the most of his opportunity. He did what everyone (who is successful) practices. He networked. He made it a point to do more than just pick up his flyers. He met the key people from the Warner Bros. publicity and promotion department, because in the back of his mind he was planning to dump his legal career (despite his parent's protests) and head for Hollywood. Those names and acquaintances would be a significant help when he arrived.

"Don't expect anyone to suddenly give you a job, though," he says. "When I went to Hollywood, I did not anticipate that. I did, however, have a plan."

Olds' plan was not much different from one that someone would utilize if they were unemployed and looking for a job. "When I hit Hollywood and visited the people at Warners, my sole goal was to get them to give me the names of five additional people I could ask for employment. I didn't really expect to land a job at Warners, but if it happened, great. But, I did want five references from every studio person I met. If I got that, I knew I could not miss."

HOW TO USE REFERENCES

Olds had another thing going with the references. The fact they were references. "When you can use someone's name and tell the person you are calling you were referred by so and so, it has tremendous impact. It is no longer a cold call." Olds is right. Major corporations think the same way when they search for a new employee. Any person who applies that has a reference from a present employee usually gets special treatment, and most of the time the position.

"Most people," he says, "will give you references if you ask. They want to be helpful, especially if they have had some experience with you. When we were on campus, I worked hard, never sloughed off, and always gave WB their money's worth. They remembered that when I visited the studio."

Olds stood out in the WB executives' mind for other reasons. He was always "up," never depressed or down. "Everyone likes to be around positive people. No one wants to associate with someone who is depressed (unless, of course, they are depressed as well)." Olds scored high in the studio executives' mind.

Olds walked away from WB's Burbank studios with the names of five other executives who might help him in some way. "All I needed was for one door to open from among those five."

Olds recommends another technique. Send a handwritten note whether they give you a job or not. It's a great touch. "In this business—in fact, in every business—you never know when you are going to run across someone again. People move up and down, quickly. Today's assistant producer might be tomorrow's director. I wanted everyone to remember me in a positive manner."

How to Use Notes

Olds sent the notes. "That's a nice touch that few people practice, but it can be enormously important. Contacts," says Olds, "is the name of this business. You don't get anywhere in entertainment without knowing someone and building relationships." Placement specialists and human resource directors agree. Whether it is a thank you note for an interview, or just a few lines showing someone's appreciation for a referral, it can be a critically important part of the job hunting process.

Mark Denis, a voice-over announcer who has been extremely successful, has a simple technique he developed in order to keep in touch with people. He tracks everyone's birth date, and calls them on that day to wish them happy birthday. Olds did not go to that extreme, but he remembered the notes and for a good reason. One of those WB references led to an interview and a job offer from Minot Entertainment, a small publicity and promotion firm that worked with Orion Pictures. They liked Olds, his background, and the WB references he brought with him. Most important, they hired him for $650 a week.

"I didn't know much about promoting and publicizing pictures, but I was willing to work hard and learn. I think they were impressed by what I had done at college for WB, and the fact WB was willing to recommend me." At Minot, Olds did everything. That's expected of every newcomer. "Just because I was making a good wage did not mean I could not operate the Xerox."

Olds learned things besides publicity and promotion at Minot—"never say you don't want to do it, and do everything with a smile." It wasn't long before Olds was handling some of Minot's major accounts and promoting some of the most important films coming out of Hollywood.

"Promotion is not difficult," says Olds. It is simply a matter of getting news of your product out and known to those who may buy it. In non-entertainment terms, it could take the form of McDonald's running 2-for-1 Big Mac discount coupons. Or, on a more sophisticated level, it might take the form of a major newspaper interviewing and running a story on Leonardo DiCaprio. DiCaprio's promoter (or the promoter who represents the studio that is producing a film with DiCaprio as star) goes to the media (newspaper, magazine, etc.) and gives the editors a "hook" or "angle" for a story. It might be "how DiCaprio views his new role as compared to the one he had in *Titanic* and how they differ."

What's Behind the Stories

Hooks and angles are the basis of stories that consumers would like to read, see or hear about. The promoter could present the angle to the (print) press, or propose it to *Entertainment Tonight* for an interview, or suggest it to David Letterman's producers as a guest. If you examine today's newspaper, especially the entertainment section, most of the stories have hooks and angles.

Olds was taught to develop them to expose the clients (motion pictures) that Minot represented. Despite the fact it paid well, a promotional career was not his ultimate goal. He wasn't sure what he wanted, he recalls, "but I knew I did not want to spend my career in promotion. I had other ideas."

Craig Miller had ideas, too, but they weren't about entertainment. Miller was in school majoring in liberal arts, and heading for a career as a psychologist, but he was detoured by a love of science fiction. Miller, who later became the producer of some of the most successful animated cartoon series in Hollywood, was a science fiction buff, a genre that had not, as yet become big in Hollywood.

But the science fiction bug bit him solidly. He was such a buff that he attended virtually every sci fi conference and meeting that was held in southern California. At one of those gatherings, he ran into a group of publicity and promotional people who were working for a then, unknown, studio that was being established by George Lucas. The studio was searching for talent to help them promote their first major venture, a motion picture called *Star Wars*. Miller was the perfect fit. He knew the field and was well aware of how to do science fiction "niche marketing." In other words promote *Star Wars* to science fiction buffs.

Miller had read all the science fiction publications, knew when and where the conferences were held, and was also aware of what niche publications the science fiction fans read. Lucas was searching for someone with Miller's qualifications. He wanted to reach every possible science fiction fan in the country and was not sure that typical motion picture advertisements would do the job.

Lucas wanted to cover every possible base, and although it is difficult to imagine *Star Wars* flopping, before the release and the initial box office receipts were registered, there was always that chance. Lucas wanted to reach every market segment, and Miller's ability to reach the science fiction fans was a critical component of the Star Wars marketing plan.

NICHE MARKETING—HOW IT WORKS

In today's motion picture promotion campaigns, it is usually the masses—the general audiences that are targeted. They are reached through newspapers, magazines, television, and radio. But studios know there are extra dollars that can be had, and nearly every entertainment production (motion picture, television, stage) has a niche that holds additional potential attendees. *Cocoon*—a motion picture about aging seniors—was promoted to general audiences (through daily newspapers) but could also be promoted to the senior crowd through such (senior) niche publications as the AARP magazine.

Niche marketing is not new in entertainment. For instance, mystery motion pictures can be promoted to audiences through mystery magazines. Comedies through such television shows such as Jay Leno or the half-hour situation comedies on television. That does not mean the film or television series cannot be promoted outside the niche, however, the niche adds to the total promotion plan.

Although Miller had never had a promotion course, he became adept in the art because he recognized the basics. First, promotion is not a skill that takes someone years to learn. If it does, they are probably not good promoters to start. The best promoters are usually those who use their instinct and common sense to reach people. They are also people who believe in their product. If they don't, they know they cannot sell it to anyone. You cannot shove a film—or product—down anyone's throat if they do not like it. In the record industry there is a saying, one that describes the difficulties of marketing something that the audience does not want—"You can't hype a stiff." In other words, if the audience will not buy it, if they do not like it, regardless of how much (promotion) money you spend, you will not be able to sell it.

There are hundreds of examples of entertainment products that were produced for exorbitant costs and promoted with an equal amount of money, yet they did not make it because the public would not buy. Motion pictures like Ishtar which turned out to be multimillion dollar flops despite the funds that were spent on them.

FLOPS AND TIMING

Promotion is a key behind-the-scenes positon (job). Perhaps the all-time classic promotion story comes out of the record industry.

It revolves around one of the most popular groups that ever recorded—the Beatles—and the first hit they had in this country, "I Want to Hold Your Hand," which became a multimillion seller, established the group, and revolutionized the record industry.

What few realize, however, is that "Hand" was not the first recording released in the United States by the British foursome. "Hand," which was released on December 26, 1963, was preceded by a half-dozen songs, all released in 1962 and early 1963. Not one of the songs sold more than 35 copies, nor did they ever garner any airplay. The public was not ready to buy.

What happened? No one really knows why those records did not sell, but everyone knows what made the Beatles a national phenomena. Right after "I Want to Hold Your Hand" was released, one of their promotion specialists convinced Ed Sullivan—who had the leading variety show on television—to have the foursome on as a guest. Sullivan, who had never heard of the group, agreed when he saw their picture (Remember? They had long hair and looked odd). When the Beatles appeared in February 1964, the reaction was so great, that Sullivan booked them for two additional appearances. The rest, of course, is history. "Hand" went on to sell millions, and every one of those six records that had been previously released and flopped, were re-released and sold millions as well, too.

What was the secret? Timing. The country was not ready for the foursome in 1962 and early 1963, but in late 1963 and early 1964, America was recovering from a trauma—the assassination of President John F. Kennedy. Consumers were looking for something light, good humored, and cheerful. The Beatles filled the bill.

TIMING IS EVERYTHING

In entertainment timing is everything. When *Star Wars* was released, consumers were ready for a good, high quality, science fiction film. But, the promoter has to guess right, and correctly judge the pulse of the consumers. Good promoters are good salespeople. They take a product and bring it to the attention of the audience that is going to buy it, or they might grab the consumer's attention with flyers or stories in specialized magazines.

Being thrust into the promotion field may have been one of the best things for Miller and Olds. They learned about consumer tastes, likes, and dislikes. They also learned how to reach them and the importance of marketing. That early promotion experience aided both later when Olds had the opportunity to create a television series and Miller got involved in animation. They learned that creativity is a critical ingredient in entertainment, but creating just to be creative, without knowing if there is an audience for a product, can be a waste of time.

So, where does someone go if they start off in the promotion field? There are dozens of promotion and PR firms in Hollywood—as well as other cities throughout the country—that are willing to have interns or "gophers." Starting in production does not mean one has to stay there. Neither Miller or Olds had visions of making promotion a permanent occupation.

But promotion can be extremely lucrative. For three years Miller promoted Lucas' films, and by the time *The Empire Strikes Back* was released, he had become so proficient in the field that he started his own marketing company, where he specialized in providing promotion and marketing services for other motion picture companies. Miller generated one client after another, and for a good reason—he had a track record. In entertainment, as in any other industry, your past performance becomes an indicator of your future efforts. Those in entertainment are judged heavily by their past performance. Whether it is as a messenger or director, what you did and how you did it counts.

During the next six years, Miller promoted a variety of films, but like Olds, he was not convinced that marketing was his bailiwick. In the back of his mind he had other goals. "PR and promotion are tough," he says. "That doesn't mean there isn't opportunity, but you are constantly trying to convince people— consumers and the media—that there is value in the product you are representing. It's an exciting aspect of the business, but like anything else it can be draining. You must always come up with new ideas and approaches, and, you are always promoting someone else's work. I wanted to do my own."

THE CRITICAL ELEMENT

"I wanted to create products and have someone else promote them for me." Although Miller did not have anything specific in mind, his career took a turn (for the better) thanks to one thing—networking. "I can't stress how important networking is for anyone. Someone I knew was story editing an animated series. They had 65 half hours they had to do, and they gave me an opportunity to write an episode." Miller had never written one before, but he had skills as a writer. Whereas in many industries, Miller might have been permanently pigeonholed as a promotion man, one of the major pluses of the entertainment field is that you can move from one position to another, from one occupation to another.

Chuck Bowman, who started in the business by applying at NBC for a page's (messenger) job, moved from one occupation to another. Although the page position did not pay much, Bowman was able to use it to create a career. "Most of the entry level positions do not pay well," says Bowman, "but they frequently have advantages." One was working in the studio where Bowman was able to use the facilities. He did not waste time, either. One afternoon he put together a radio demonstration tape, and sent it to his hometown (10,000 watt) station in hopes of landing a job. "Demos are a must if you intend to get anything in radio or commercials."

Unfortunately—or was it fortunately—Bowman's hometown station turned him down, but suggested another station in a town (Hays) not far away. Bowman sent the tape and landed a position. "I worked every shift and job imaginable. In a smaller market with a small station you have more learning opportunities," he says. "That was one of the beauties in working in Hays. I wasn't ready for a network, and I needed to hone my skills as well as learn others. If you start on a network affiliate in a major market, you seldom get the chance to do the things I did. If you are an associate producer, you wind up running errands all the time . . . and doing nothing else. But, if you luck out and get to a smaller market where they do not have an abundance of staff, you frequently find yourself doing a number of things and truly learning."

In Hays, Bowman learned everything. It gave him the chance to get involved in television, since the owners of the radio station were building a TV outlet. That does not happen to frequently in a large market. Thus, Bowman went from radio announcer and deliverer of commercials, announcements, etc. to the television outlet where he did everything from hosting a kids cartoon show (he also got his first shot at directing) to reporting sports and weather. From there he moved to Tulsa and a bigger television station where he did the late night movie, weather, and a Saturday afternoon show.

OPPORTUNITY IN SMALLER MARKETS

Bowman was only beginning. His hope was to get back to Hollywood—and he did—where he worked for Stephen J. Cannell, one of television's most prolific creators, and became associate producer (Baa Baa Blacksheep), director (Incredible Hulk and V) and an Emmy award winner. None of that would have been possible had he not had the opportunity to learn and grow in a market that was not big.

Bowman's rise offers an excellent lesson to those eyeing the industry. Don't forget smaller markets. It is often easier to get started in one. In smaller stations management is not as constrained as in major markets. The smaller market stations can afford to take chances, since they are usually not in a life-and-death battle for ratings and numbers. In major markets, they are and any personnel moves are colored by what they believe their ratings will do. Thus, in many major markets they will not hire certain on-air personalities because they do not fit the desires of their audience profile.

Bowman's versatility is typical of those who make it in the business. Miller traveled a similar route. After the first animated episode he wrote, he met Michael Tracvinski, a story editor. The two hit it off and ultimately Tracvinski went on to create one of the most popular syndicated sci fi shows on television, *Babylon 5*. The combination of the relationship and Miller's talents soon opened the doors for Craig in numerous other areas.

Is there a blueprint that Miller has that can be followed? Or, how about Bowman and Olds? No, all took similar roads—they started out wherever they could—and learned. Perhaps the best explanation is given by special effects pro Brick Price, a 25-year veteran of the business. "Entertainment is a unique industry. Take, for instance, the film companies. Compared to aerospace (where he worked prior to entertainment), film is loosely structured. It's similar to a band of gypsies. If, for instance, I was to look at the typical aerospace resume, it would have someone's employment as something like 27 years for Hughes or some other company. The key is they would have a long record of employment for one company.

"But, if you saw a film resume, it would jump around. Most jobs would be for less than a year. If the aerospace human resource (HR) director looked at it, they would be shocked. If the HR person in the film industry examined it, they would be pleased. Just think about how these two industries differ and you can see what's important when people go job hunting.

WHAT FILM THRIVES ON

"Aerospace thrives on stability and teamwork. Working together. Film thrives on creativity, the flash and brilliance of creative people. Creative people do not necessarily work for a long time in one spot. That's one thing you should never be concerned about in this business—hopping around. All of us do it."

Miller and Olds weren't the only ones who were able to get a foot in the door by starting with promotion. Andy Epstein, a dual Emmy winner, always wanted to be a writer in the entertainment field, but his journalist father steered him away from the written word and to promotion. Andy was not sold on the area, but he took the plunge anyhow.

He started where many other promotion people began—the mailroom of Bob Levinson's public relations/promotion firm. Levinson is not the only promotion person to offer opportunities to newcomers. There are dozens of promotion and public relations' firms in every city that either look for interns or are searching for someone to work in the mailroom. But, if anyone is going to apply for those positions, it would be wise to remember to be "up" and interested. Learn something about the company before applying. For instance, it is relatively easy to call and ask a receptionist or secretary in what area the promotion firm specializes and what clientele they have.

Know something about the company before seeing a hiring manager. Be prepared to ask a question or two. It shows the hiring manager you're interested and have taken the time to look into the firm. It also says you are interested in more than just finding a job. Most people who apply for positions don't take the time to find those things out. Yet, a little knowledge can mean the difference between someone getting the position and not getting it. Imagine if you had your own company and were interviewing people for a position. Suppose two candidates came in and one knew nothing about your enterprise, nor did they ask any questions. On the other hand, the other person was curious, had knowledge of what your company did, and some of the clients you had. Which would you hire?

WHO YOU KNOW COUNTS

Although Epstein had demonstrated his writing skills through features he had written that appeared in school newspapers, the fact his father knew promotion specialist Bob Levinson did not hurt when the younger Epstein interviewed for the job.

Epstein was hired and moved quickly from the mailroom into a promotional spot in the firm. Within a short time, he was writing press releases, artist biographies ("we handled a lot of entertainment clients") and trying to sell (pitch) stories on clients to the media.

"I had trouble with the pitching (selling) part," he recalls. "I never felt at home with it." Still, Epstein proved to be an excellent writer and developed into a top promotion specialist. If he had not, the connection between his father and Levinson would not have mattered. Contacts are critical and can open the doors, but then it is up to you to deliver. Epstein did.

Working for Levinson had its advantages. Epstein learned the entertainment business inside-out, but he wanted to get back to entertainment journalism. After 18 months, he left Levinson and approached the editor of *Calendar*, the *Los Angeles Times* entertainment magazine, with a story idea. Epstein recalls the difficulty he had. "To walk into a major newspaper and actually meet with the editors was intimidating. But the editor liked my idea and gave me the assignment. It took me a long time to write that first story, but eventually I finished. He liked it so much that he began to give me additional assignments."

Not all the stories were strictly entertainment. Epstein found that *Calendar* was going from "more soft pieces to harder, investigative pieces." Working on exposés soon brought him to the attention of Public Broadcasting System (PBS), where he did a series on the financial mismanagement of a local television station.

GOOD INVESTIGATIVE TECHNIQUES

Gossip columnist Rona Barrett, who had a segment on *Good Morning, America*, spotted Epstein, liked his writing and investigative abilities, and hired him to assist on her daily, 5-minute television segment. Once again, the ability to do more than one thing—write in more than one style—opened the doors for Epstein to other assignments and opportunities. The switch was not easy, though. From 5000 word articles, Epstein had to condense his reports to 30 words (for Barrett). Television is a sound bite medium. Whereas, magazines (i.e., *Calendar*) want longer pieces. When you try to reach a television audience, the best (and most effective) way to do it through short, quick, sound bites: 30 words or 15 seconds. Being able to do both is one reason why Epstein's career soared. It is also an example of how important it is to avoid being pigeonholed. The broader the talents you are perceived to have, the greater the chance you have to climb the ladder.

With credits like *Good Morning, America*, Epstein's reputation and his versatile writing style became known throughout the industry. He was hired by *Entertainment Tonight*, the "E" channel to create programming (he created eight shows). He even designed and put together the channel's news department. Epstein was never typecast as "one kind of writer or editor." The versatility he displayed enabled him to go on and become one of the top editors and producers in the business. "The key," he says, "is once you get a chance in the business, don't screw it up."

"Work hard," says Don Graham, "and you'll make it. If you do, you're bound to have alot of success—as well as fun."

How Most Define Their
Entertainment Experience

Fun is the way most in the business define their experiences. "If you can't have fun doing this stuff, don't. And, if you don't have enthusiasm for it, get out." Graham has always viewed his job as one that has to be fun. "Initially, I never asked about a salary, and it was years before I did. The prime criteria for a job in this business is do you enjoy it? It has to be fun or else you could never work the long hours, weekends, and handle the traveling."

Graham's enthusiasm wasn't lost on a drugstore owner named Russ Solomon. Graham met Solomon years ago and, at the time, he knew little about entertainment but had enormous energy and enthusiasm. "Solomon was planning to split part of the drugstore (called Tower Drugs) and carry records. He needed help and asked me to organize it. Within four days I did, and then Solomon made a decision. He completely discarded all the drug items, made the entire thing a record store, and called it Tower Records." Solomon offered Graham $200 a month to start. His job was "everything from stocking records to building shelves. I didn't care, I loved the business and wanted to be in it."

Although Graham, Miller, Olds, and Epstein seem to have entertainment industry positions that are worlds apart, there is a common denominator, once again, in their rise—connections count and so does daring, the willingness to go out on a limb and try something different. As a rule, if you are searching for security, the entertainment business is not for you.

There are exceptions. Brick Price says it depends upon the level to which you want to go. "If you just want to work for Disney—and there is nothing wrong with that—and collect a payroll check, in my end of the business you could probably do that. But, if you want to do your own thing, create your own company and build it, you have to take a chance. Remember, though, that the smaller companies tend to come and go."

Interestingly, nearly all the entertainment business people in this book are doing their own thing. They may have worked for someone at one time, but in the end, to take the major creative leap, most have wound up working for themselves. They are risk takers and with the daring of a Graham or Tom Sanders, the stuntman/photographer/cinematographer.

Sanders, who has been involved in 95 percent of all the skydiving stunts you see in motion pictures, tossed his fear of heights aside and created a business by taking pictures of other jumpers as they left the airplane. "It might sound silly," he says, "but I thought they take pictures of us at the prom so why not the first time we jump out of an airplane?" For Sanders, it was a matter of finding a niche and filling it.

WHERE YOU GET THE OPPORTUNITY

Miller tossed aside a promising career as a psychologist, while photojournalist Les Rose gave up on medicine to become an intern at a local television station. "Intern," advises Rose, "at the small stations. That's where you get the opportunity to do things. During my internship I had the chance to write and edit stories on the weekend at the station. That's an incredible break, and it opened up my entire career."

Special assignment editor, Richard Alvarez, has taken his share of risks, too. His initial job—as a messenger—almost turned into a dead end. For 18 months, Alvarez toiled at the station, running errands, handling laundry, getting lunch for whomever, and doing whatever needed to be done. Alvarez started to lose some of his zeal and confidence when he found that the manager of the Electronic News Gathering (ENG) service at the station had passed him up twice for a promotion. There is nothing more devastating than losing one's confidence, especially in a business where you are responsible for making difficult choices (which show, which picture, which take, should you choose).

Then the ENG manager gave Alvarez his break. He remembers it well. "It was a recycling story, and my entire family was around the television set that night to watch my first 20-second segment."

After that it moved fast for Alvarez. He spent eight years with his partner, and traveled throughout the country shooting everything from sports to travel features. "Sure, I took a risk in giving up the stable, librarian job, but you have to realize that whatever career you choose, you are going to be doing it the rest of your life. I tried to envision myself as a librarian for the next 25 years, and it wasn't appealing. But I could see myself traveling around and shooting news and feature events for television."

HOW TO SEE FROM ANOTHER PERSPECTIVE

Alvarez, like many others, owes part of his success to the fact he is an original thinker. He's creative and can see things differently or from another perspective. One of the foundations of the entertainment business is creativity, the ability to put a new twist on something old. Once you establish a reputation for creativity, the opportunities come to you. Graham was that way, and his reputation grew, partly because of the unique ways he did things.

What Graham did with A&M Records is a perfect example. Most remember that Herb Alpert and Jerry Moss were the two founding figures, but the role that Graham played was critical. Long before he helped A&M, Graham's innovative ideas had impacted the record and entertainment field.

From his base in San Francisco, he was instrumental in developing the "rack jobber" concept. That is, he would visit retail locations that did not carry records, and offer to put in racks that held the top 40 tunes. Each week he would come through, restock and change the top 40 records. The retailer did not have to do anything because Graham's crew did it all the stocking and work. Although the sight of racks is common in the industry today, when Graham entered the business it was not being done.

One of the interesting things about Graham's program was that his "stocking crew" was not what most would imagine. First, Graham—with suit and tie—would make a call on a major retailer (i.e., Woolworth). He would sell them on the concept of the rack and the top 40 tunes, and as soon as he got the signature on a contract, he would head out to the alley where he parked his truck, took off his coat and tie and immediately walked the rack back into the store with the stock—before anyone could change their mind. A one-man operation? Not quite, but it is indicative of the type of original thinking that Graham put into the ventures in which he was involved. Working with artists and pounding on the doors of radio stations to get product played is not easy, but few were as successful as Graham.

WHAT THE PUBLIC WILL NOT BUY

"I always kept in mind what the radio station needed as well as what the consumers would like. I never tried to push a record that I did not believe in because ultimately, even if you get it played on the radio station and stocked in stores, the public will not buy it."

There might, however, be one exception in Graham's history. Once, he recalls, he was doing promotion for Warner Bros. which, at the time, was a relatively new label. One day a record arrived by Ed "Kookie" Byrnes, an actor who had developed an enormous (female) following because of the television show he was on, 77 *Sunset Strip*.

Although Byrnes did not sing the best, the label still released the cut. "It was," recalls Graham laughing, "a rotten cut. But the label wanted to get it into the hands of radio stations and that was my job. I sincerely doubted if it ever would be played."

Graham took the record to the number one station in town (KOBY, San Francisco). He gave the program director the cut and instead of playing the "A" (chosen) side, the director flipped it to the "B" side where a tune called "Kookie, Kookie Lend Me Your Comb" was recorded. Graham cringed but the program director "flipped over it. He said I was right, it was an absolute smash. I tried to tell him he was playing the wrong side, but he wouldn't listen. He slapped the record on the air immediately and the telephone lines rang off the hook with consumers calling and telling him how much they loved it. Ultimately, the record became a smash hit."

Successes like "Kookie" kept Graham in and on top of the business. Although he had numerous opportunities to give up the promotion tag and become an executive, Graham has always stuck "where the fun is . . . that's the only way to be in this business."

Stuntman Sanders is as much of an opportunist as Graham. "All these people were jumping out of airplanes, some for the first time, and they rarely had any record of it. That's when I got the idea—why not take pictures as they jump and sell it to them."

That's when Sanders started shooting. He used everything from stills to video and 16 mm. The business grew, and before long his reputation as an aerial photographer soared. Celebrities came out to jump, and Sanders shot them. From there, it wasn't long before the stars were talking about his ability and producers and directors began to use him for skydiving shots and stunts.

Sanders became one of four skydiving cinematographers in the country, and today is involved in 95 percent of all the skydiving shots that are shown in films. The other thing that set both Sanders and Graham apart was word-of-mouth. They became noted as two people who not only did the job, but did it creatively as well.

Don't Wait When You See Opportunity

Sanders built his business and succeeded because he saw an opportunity. Opportunities do not come along that often, but when they do "don't wait, take advantage of them," says Graham. "Always use your creativity, too," says Graham. "Try to do things a little differently. If it works, people will remember."

"Twinkle" is an excellent example of how Graham—and others—do things differently. "Twinkle" was the first cut produced by a new label out of Los Angeles. They called Graham in San Francisco and asked for his promotional help. The label had little money, and the artist was a part-time actor who was crazy about bullfighting. His partner told Graham that "Twinkle" was not finished. They were going to add crowd noises from a bull-fight and change the name.

Graham had heard similar stories and forgot about it. But, a few weeks later the new record arrived, complete with bullfight and crowd noise, a new title, and a new name for the artists as well. "It was sensational," recalls Graham. "It had a live feel to it. I ran up the hill to the number one station in town. At the time, this station had a number of on-air personalities, and they could play whatever they wanted."

But, the disk jockey crew was selective. They would listen to the record and play it, however, if it turned out to be a stiff—with little or no audience reaction—"they would not invite you back for awhile," says Graham. Graham was willing to take the chance. He thought the record was great and the telephones would ring off the hook. Within minutes he was at the station. In one hand was the record, in the other a bag with burgers and milkshakes in it.

THE MAKING OF HERB ALPERT

"I told him the name. It was called 'The Lonely Bull' by Herb Alpert and the Tijuana Brass. Without hesitating he frowned and told me 'we don't play Mexican music.'"

"I told him it wasn't typical mariachi music or anything similar. So, he took the record, slapped it on the turntable, and within minutes after the song was finished every telephone line lit up. We had a smash. Between 12 noon and 3 P.M. that day he played it more than a dozen times."

Graham called Jerry Moss, the other half of the A(Alpert) & M (Moss). There was only one problem—Moss did not have any records pressed, he was short of funds. Graham instantly began to make telephone calls to distributors in the area. News of the reaction to the record had spread throughout the city, and every distributor wanted copies—which Graham said he could deliver if the distributor paid for the record, in advance.

Paying in advance had never been done before. All records were given to distributors on consignment, and the distributor could return any he wanted for full refund or credit. Graham was changing the rules. He wanted cash upfront. The record was so hot, that Graham was able to get away with it. Every distributor paid in advance, and later that afternoon Graham picked up the checks, and sent them overnight to Moss so he could press records and pay for the manufacturing.

That record—and approach—put A&M Records in business. Credit the success to Graham who not only got the record played but put the label on sound financial footing at the same time. "Call it taking advantage of an opportunity," smiles Graham.

Opportunity put photojournalist Les Rose on the map, too. It wasn't as elaborate as Graham's ploy, but it did put an intern (Rose) on the road to five Emmys. At the time, Rose had landed his first job in the entertainment business. He had become an intern for one of the leading television stations in Tampa, Florida.

THE TECHNOLOGY IMPACT

Les, an outgoing, genial, aggressive journalist, was able to do more than cut copy and run errands for the station. Working weekends, the station allowed Rose to shoot, write, and edit news stories that came up over the two day period. Aside from the experience, Rose benefitted because of technology. The year he became a television intern, stories were being phased out on film and video was coming into play. Thus, he not only garnered film experience but video as well.

"It was a great learning experience, " he says. "Video, which does not have any processing, was replacing film. Thus, for the first time, news could be instantaneous. Every station went to video, and I was fortunate to be in the middle of the changeover. They not only gave me the opportunity to shoot and write, but learn a new format."

It also taught Rose something else—"keep your eye out for new developments and be willing to do anything to help further your career, regardless of how insignificant it might seem. You never know what you are going to pick up." In fact, none of Rose's television exposure would have been possible were it not for another internship he served the year before. As a junior in college, he spent six months on a radio station. Although it was on campus, Rose was able to learn the ins and outs of writing copy and editing for radio.

"It wasn't television, but it gave me the basic journalism experience. I learned a great deal about the impact of sound—that's how you have to think about radio—and how important it was to the story. By spending six months with that assignment, I learned enough of the basics to be able to edit television film on the weekends. A lot of kids might not be willing to spend time on a campus radio station, I did. You never know what is going to pay off. For me, it was that simple internship. It could be something equally as mundane for someone else trying to get into the business. The key is to take advantage of every opportunity."

Internships, points out Rose, are critically important. "Don't just be satisfied being an intern and following directions. Find yourself a mentor, someone who likes you. Ask them questions, get advice. It's amazing what you can learn from them and how they will help you. I was friends with the weekend news anchors, Bob Hite, and Gayle Sierens. I learned an incredible amount from them, and because of the things they helped me with the doors opened."

Bill Royce is in complete agreement with Rose. "If you want to get into television, become an intern on any TV show," he says. "It isn't as difficult as you may think. Write to the shows, tell them you want to become an intern. Ask them if they need any kind of help. Just forget about titles and money. That will come later. Once you do, you can make the decision as to what job you want. Talent coordinator, producer, whatever. The key is to first get your foot in the door."

How to Land Internship

How and where do you land internships? Erick Finke knows. The website producer built his career on internships, and says there is no better place to find one than with some of the local cable television outlets.

"Many have to provide local programming, and they look for volunteers to help put video together. Through local cable, you can learn almost everything there is to know about film/video. That was one of the places I learned. The only drawback is there isn't much in the way of compensation."

Finke points out two ways to get video training. There are numerous film companies and production houses in every town—regardless of the size—that are amenable to volunteers. That's where Finke first learned video and also discovered that "my skills were not in the directorial vein." A second avenue is local cable channels. Most have to provide a certain amount of local programming, and they do not want to spend money. Hence, they are open to volunteers to not only spend time at the station but actually create programming.

Finke found a station that was committed to putting on eight shows a year for the local community. Along with his partner, he volunteered, they were hired, and immediately thrown into the station and named "floor managers." Floor managers are usually on-stage, talking to (via headsets) and taking directions from the director.

"That's a potent way to learn," says Finke. "You are working with the director, and you begin to learn his rationale for doing things." Within three months, Finke was directing and producing local shows. From there he became an assistant director, the person who sits next to the director and executes the orders as they are given.

"It was great training," says Erick. 'Nowhere could you have received the tutoring that we did. It did not pay, but it was worth a million dollars. That same opportunity is open to virtually everyone if they have a local cable outlet. Volunteer. You'd be amazed and what you'll wind up doing and learning."

THE CABLE OPPORTUNITY

Although it appears that finding an opening might be difficult, Finke points out that most people trying to break into the business go to a major studio, a network affiliate or a large independent channel. Few try the cable outlets because they want to start near the top. Cable is a great opportunity. They are short-handed and short of budget. The perfect combination for someone who wants to break into the business.

Regardless of where someone goes, there is no right or wrong way to break into the business. Internships get high marks from everyone. If they are interested in promotion, there are dozens of promotion firms in every city that would consider taking on an intern, especially one they did not have to pay. The same is true of personal management and agencies, film and video enterprises, or any entertainment occupation.

Remember, however, the pay will be minimal (if at all) but the knowledge is worth a college education. There is a caveat, however. Small, independent firms may shy away from internships if they think they have to pay. They look upon interns as novices who have little or no ability, and do not have the budgets larger companies possess. Consequently, why put out any money—even if it is minimal—if they will get little in return. Then, there are some outlets that may have to put aside monies to hire interns as part of their contract with a city or other local government. The prospective entertainment industry employee has to look at these firms and agencies objectively.

Volunteering also means you may wind up doing everything from changing lightbulbs and running the copy machine to fetching lunch and taking the boss's clothing to the cleaners. Bowman says no two internships (or break-in positions) will be the same. "This is not a cookie cutter business. Everything differs, all jobs vary. There are no set standards and few job descriptions that pinpoint exactly what you will do. But every job is a learning experience. Remember, too, even if you get turned down for a position or one of your ideas is discarded, that is not a reflection on your ability. A friend of mine," he says, "could not get a job in the business, but he thought he would make a great scriptwriter. No one believed him, but he was determined. He stuck to it and finished the script and sold it. It was *Brave Heart.*"

THE STREISAND LEGEND

The entertainment business is rife with stories of talented people who are turned down and have a difficult time breaking into the business. Legend has it that Barbra Streisand was turned down by one opinionated label producer who said he would not sign her because "she sang through her nose." The Beatles were turned down more than once by Capitol Records because label executives thought they sounded too much like "old time" rock and roll.

Entertainment is fraught with disappointments—and successes. It is not a business where you take an exam and automatically qualify. This is not like Jet Propulsion Laboratory where everyone has a similar background. In entertainment, people come from all walks of life, and the better ones think creatively and differently.

Photojournalist Richard Alvarez adds that this is a business of breaks. "You have to know people. That's the only way they are going to hire you. I don't mean kissing someone's rear end, but make sure people know who you are. Especially if you are a messenger and you're hoping to move up. Let someone know about your dreams. Be visible. There are always openings, but you'll never get one if people don't know you want it."

Bob Schulenberg was going to be a painter before he was bitten by the bug. One thing that gave him an extraordinary background was the film experience he had in college. "It won't land you a job, but you can learn a great deal." Schulenberg, who went to UCLA, did a 5-minute animated film in working toward a masters in animation. He wrote, directed, and conceived the entire production. "Hands on can't be replaced. You get some real knowledge of how a film is put together. Anything you can do along those lines is a plus."

Schulenberg, who always wanted to be in film, entered the business in an unusual way. One day after graduation, he met the costume designer for MGM studios. One thing led to another and the designer suggested that Schulenberg put together a portfolio. For those who do have experience, a portfolio is a must. Finke had a thick one that originated when he was doing work for the local cable station.

OBJECT OF A PORTFOLIO

Schulenberg's portfolio, however, was a problem. He had not worked in the business previously, so where could he start? That's when the idea hit him. The portfolio was a chance to show how creative and capable he was. He took a well-known play, designed costumes for the characters and even indicated which fabric would go with the costumes. Al Nickel, who headed Western Costume, saw Schulenberg's work and was overwhelmed by it. Although, Schulenberg had not landed any work, his portfolio showed what he could do. Nickel hired him immediately. "It was a spec job," Schulenberg says, "and I knew no one was going to pay for it, but sometimes you have to take a chance."

Peter Lefcourt took numerous chances in his quest for a screenwriting career, but along the way he figured out how to break into television and sell scripts. Lefcourt, whose experience was almost entirely confined to short stories for magazines, made a study of television. He watched it day and night to get the flavor of how things are done. He was broke, living in Venice (California) and "we were so poor we did not even have

an answering service (this was in the day before machines became popular). We all left our doors open, and if someone heard
the telephone ring, they would answer it for the other person.

THE FIRST STEP IN SELLING SCRIPT

"We were all trying to sell stuff to television—or to anyone. I
thought the best way to do that was make a study of it (television). And I did. Some things immediately became obvious.
Everything has to be fast moving, forget the cerebral stuff." Lefcourt, who won an Emmy for *Cagney & Lacey*, the detective series,
likes television as a writer's medium because the "writer controls the episode. That's unlike motion pictures, where the
script is usually taken out of your hands, someone rewrites it
and you have little control."

Regardless of which route a writer takes—motion pictures
or television—Lefcourt says "study. It may seem silly, but you
would be amazed at how much you can learn about television
series and motion pictures by simply watching. Watching is the
first step to selling a script."

Whether someone is selling a script or trying to become a
talent coordinator. Olds says to remember that this is a people
business. When he knocked on Nancy Kirkpatrick's door he did
not come away with a job, but he had something almost as valuable, referrals—that is, the names of others who might place
him. "That was my rule . . . if I knocked on your door and if you
did not have anything, I asked for references, for other people
you could recommend."

At Minot, where he started, Olds did everything. "You have
to . . . especially when you are the newcomer. Just because I was
making $650 a week did not mean I could not operate the copy
machine—and I did." Olds' credits his work ethic ("never say
you don't want to do it, and do everything with a smile") with
moving quickly up the company ladder. Before long, he was handling some of Minot's major promotion accounts."

How do you train for a promotion position? "I don't think you do. My entire background was passing out flyers, but if you are enthusiastic about your product (whether it be a film or something else) that enthusiasm is going to be catchy. The audience you are trying to reach recognizes that."

Olds also absorbed a great deal. "I had limited promotion knowledge, but working with people who had spent years in the profession rubs off. You learn."

LEARNING THE TRADE

Screenwriter Peter Lefcourt learned, too. "Wherever you want to go in this business you have to learn the skill or trade. Most of the time it is not something you can take in college. Mine wasn't."

Initially, Lefcourt, who had hopes of breaking into television (or motion pictures) as a screenwriter, remembers when he came to Hollywood in the early 1970s in "an old VW with a few dollars in my pocket." Lefcourt called agents and that's when he found the Catch-22.

"Agents are interested in you when you make your first sale, but you really need them before the sale—to help you make it. Unfortunately, most of the time, you cannot get one." Lefcourt recalls the first time he did get a call from an agent, which was shortly before he sold his first script. "The secretary called and then he got on the telephone. At first, I was surprised, then pleased. Unfortunately, he discovered that his secretary had dialed the wrong number. He wasn't looking for me."

But, Lefcourt was watching and studying television. "Selling a script is like any other sales process. You have to know your product," he says. "I had never watched television, perhaps because I considered myself an intellectual. However, there is no better way to learn the craft than to study it."

That's exactly what he did. "Writers have to be conscious that writing a book versus writing for television are entirely different." Television has to be fast moving and "aspiring writers are fortunate today because of the dearth of books available on television writing. When I first broke in the books weren't around."

SELLING THE IDEA

Still, Lefcourt began to master art. His first television movie idea sold, and that earned him $4,000. "Back in 1972 that was a lot of money," he says. "But then they replaced me with a string of writers. I was unhappy about it, but later I realized I probably deserved to be replaced. What they bought was the idea, not the script. They went with me for the one draft and that was it. You learn that when it comes to motion pictures or movies for television, you can lose control."

But the break was all Lefcourt needed "because I got the story credit. Because of the credit I joined the writer's guild and then got an agent. I got married too," he laughs, "and she made a good living. That was a big help, and I think most beginning writers would agree. There's nothing like a steady income, which you normally do not get in this business."

Things began to fall in place for Lefcourt. He started doing scripts for a host of television series including *Manhunter* (Ken Howard played the lead), *Kate McShane* and *Petrocelli*. "Ultimately, I was a fast study. What I saw on television, I was able to emulate. Television takes a special approach. You have to be a writer and storyteller. You need good dialogue, and you have to write concisely and visually. You have to keep all those things in mind when you're putting a script together. A television writer is more than a writer. They have to see the words and tell the story at the same time. That's different from a novel . . . frankly, I don't think William Faulkner could write for television without studying it.

"The key," says Lefcourt, "is being concise." A writer has 48 minutes to tell a story. It wasn't long before Lefcourt mastered the art and eventually won an Emmy for *Cagney & Lacey*, an hour-long police drama.

CHAPTER THREE

Climbing the Ladder

Once you get a toehold in the business, can you climb the ladder? It may be easy enough to find a job as a messenger or intern, but where does someone go after that. How do you become the Michael Ovitz of the industry, a former mailroom employee who rose to become one of the most powerful agents and executives in Hollywood. Or, for that matter, how does someone follow a trail similar to the one forged by David Geffen, another mailroom employee who went on to become one of the trio of co-owners of DreamWorks Studios?

What steps did Casey Kasem, the legendary commercial voice, follow? What formula did such award winners as Don Graham, Richard Alvarez, Les Rose, and Andy Epstein devise to get to the top? And, how do you climb when the industry is in the throes of dramatic change?

There is no simple answer to these questions. Unlike a CPA or an attorney, you don't pass an exam, work for a firm for X number of years, and then strike out on your own.

There is no set formula in the entertainment field. In corporate America, there is often a pecking order. You start at the bottom rung, get promoted, and continue to move up the ladder until you reach your limit. Most corporate employees have it planned. They know the academic degrees they will need and the steps they will have to take. Even in today's up-and-down economy, where downsizing and rightsizing have become a way of life, there is still a path that most company people can follow as they head to the top.

WHERE EVERYONE STARTS

Not so in entertainment. One thing is for sure—everyone starts at the bottom, unless their father happens to own a studio or an uncle runs a major entertainment enterprise. If they don't, they probably come up the same way Brick Price did.

Price, who founded WonderWorks, is an Emmy winner and part of the Oscar-winning team for *The Abyss*. He has built a unique enterprise and has created a highly successful special visual effects company. Like many in the entertainment field, Price's initial jobs bore no resemblance to what he ultimately ended up doing. In the military, he was a cartoonist and when he was discharged he became the technical editor of a magazine called *Model Car Science*.

How did he go on to become involved in one of the most successful special effects companies in the industry? Credit Price's drive with the fascination he had when he saw (as a youngster), *Darby O'Gill and the Little People*. The special effects were "decades ahead of the industry," he says, "and seeing the picture just sold me on the concept. I think I've seen the picture about 30 times, and I still get bowled over by it. It was so far ahead of its time."

What Price saw was a new way to do special effects. A technique that involved building miniatures differently. For instance, Price might build a miniature city, where the closest portion (to the camera lens) of whatever was going to be seen on film was large, while the remainder of the city was small, miniaturized.

One of the secrets to Price's rise was his creativity. It's a trait that he shares with the other behind-the-scenes professionals in this book.

Price's work can be complex as well as creative. "I have done," he explains, "a locomotive numerous times. It might be about four feet long, and I take it down to Union Station (in downtown Los Angeles) and shoot it as it 'goes through the wall' of the station. At the same time, you'll see people running around trying to get out of the way of the train. They are real people, the train is miniaturized, the station is life-size. The camera brings everything into perspective. Remember, the camera is a 'one-eyed idiot.' It cannot perceive depth, but through optical illusion—the Chinese mastered it 4,000 years ago and it was used nearly a half-century ago in *Darby* O'*Gill*—the train is made larger, the people smaller, and so on. That's the kind of special effects we create. It's a fascinating part of the business."

LEARN BY WATCHING OTHERS

Complex? Perhaps, but Price did not learn any of it out of a book or in a classroom. He absorbed much of it by watching *Darby* O'*Gill* and, most of all, watching others and building on what they had done. The ability to learn, absorb, and create something new and/or different is another one of those intangible requirements that is not measureable. Do you have it?

"Try to emulate others and do it better." That's what Price advises to anyone who wants to get into his end of the business. Study under someone. Watch and learn.

Price was fascinated with minatures; almost driven by them. As Graham put it, "you have to love what you're doing.

Don't get in it if you have any doubts." Price, like the others in this book, did love it. "I didn't know where I was heading, but I eventually left the magazine, and joined an advertising agency as an art director."

He moved to San Francisco with the agency, and left Hollywood far behind—so he thought. But, at the agency he began working on building models for advertisers and shooting them for advertisements. The clients were some of the best for an agency—Yamaha, Yokohama Tire, Honda, and Sontori.

Aerospace companies began to tap him for his talents. His background—building models—was ideal for putting together bids and presentations that would go to Washington for congressional meetings. The aerospace firms brought Price in for his animation skills, as well, and the last piece of the puzzle was put together when they asked him to photograph the models so they would appear full-size for hearings and meetings.

Ask Price about the training he had, and he shakes his head. "Two things made a lasting impression on me. First, when I was barely out of my teens, I entered a model building contest put on by Revell Toys. I won it, and the $1,000 that went along with it. I was floored for a couple of reasons. First, $1,000 was a lot of money then, and secondly it showed me that I was capable of doing a great deal with models. " As part of his prize, Revell continued to use him to build and photograph models for the covers of their products.

"Up until that time I never thought I was good enough for anything creative. I figured aerospace was my career, but winning the contest convinced me that I had the ability. In this business, believing in yourself is extremely important."

KEYS TO PRODUCING—EXECUTIVE PRODUCING

Erica Huggins says that executive producing and producing films often involves more than believing in yourself. "You have to know your own mind, and when you look at something know what is working: what makes the story good in the first place. You don't want to kill those elements. It is easy to be swayed and even easier to be critical of something. In fact, a producer tends to sit down with a writer and ask for changes, and frequently the changes may be just for the sake of change.

"There are many instances where you can go too far and kill the thing you liked. It has nothing to do with ego, but more than anything it involves the difficulty involved in being decisive and definitive with a creative work."

Huggins is well aware of those difficulties even though she has not been in the business that long. She's already encountered them. After *Hair Spray*, she did several motion pictures, and honed her editing skills. One film, in particular, stands out to her. Her mentors—Cort and Hampton—were involved as producers along with Scott Kroops. Huggins brought the editing skills. It was a film called *The Gun in Betty Lou's Handbag*, that was shot in Oxford, Mississippi.

Erica remembers "from the beginning, the film was a difficult shoot. You could feel it wasn't going to happen. In fact, almost anyone who has been in the editing room can tell if a film is on or off. You can feel it." The feel or intuition is what many in the business have.

Huggins' feel and intuitiveness impressed everyone that she came in contact with during her early filmmaking career. Scott and Kroops soon signed with Polygram and asked Huggins if she was interested in being a producer. The flattering offer was an example of how highly the young filmmaker was thought of, and she joined the Polygram subsidiary, Interscope, as a producer. It's also an example of how quick things can happen for someone in the business.

Huggins has given a great deal of thought to her role and believes if you want to be a successful producer, you have to be a storyteller and know how to spot a good story. "They have to find stories, they need (hopefully) good taste, how to cast, and they cannot be wishy-washy. Frankly, when I became one I wasn't even sure what a producer was supposed to do. But I did have a good understanding of films and storytelling thanks to my editing experience, and Hampton and Cort."

How to Make It

Huggins admits that she was a little concerned about the Interscope position, especially since her producing experience was not extensive. But the offer was indicative of the ability the company felt she had. Realistically, few in the business ever go from editor to producer. But Huggins brought an excitement with her. "You have to. You have to be gung-ho if you are going to make it. I realized I was lucky and had a great deal to learn. It took time, but after about three months I began to feel at home. I had an office, was reading scripts, and had a good understanding of the production process. I didn't have any doubts at that point."

Don Graham never had a problem when it came to confidence. While most people in the record business did things the traditional way, Graham lent an air of creativity and originality to everything he touched. "You need to be different. Remember, this is entertainment and people don't hire you for your accounting skills (unless, of course, they need an accountant)."

Graham, who originated the rack jobbing concept in San Francisco, climbed rapidly up the ladder. Part of the reason for the rapid rise was his outgoing, friendly manner. He loved everyone and especially what he was doing. Once you met Graham, you never forgot him. Russ Solomon, the founder of the Tower Records chain, latched onto Graham and told him he would give him $50 for each rack he could place. Graham displayed his creativity and originality from the day he entered the business.

There was a show (*Lucky Lager Dance Time*) that played the top songs each week. Graham listened to it a couple of times, and then the idea hit him. "If I knew which songs were on the top 40 beforehand, I could go to each of our racks, stack them with the 40, and then put a sign on it that said something like 'these are the songs you will hear tonight on *Lucky Lager Dance Time'*."

IMPORTANCE OF CREATIVE THINKING

With idea in hand (and his coat and tie on), Graham went to see Bill Gavin, the San Francisco music authority who programmed the top 40 for the show. Graham told him he would plug the show in every one of his locations weekly, if Gavin would give him an advance list of the top 40 so he could stock his racks. Without hesitation, Gavin agreed and "he never asked how many locations we had," recalls Graham. "We had four." Creativity. Graham had it.

Richard Alvarez, who went on to win an Emmy for his television news-producing skills, knows about creativity. After he got his initial break as a photojournalist as part of a two-man camera crew that traveled throughout north American shooting "whatever we thought was newsworthy," Alvarez began to see what it took to become a success in the business.

Alvarez discovered if you are going to be a photojournalist, you almost have to have a sixth sense for what is going to happen. When I started—about 20 years ago—television photojournalists were not commonplace. It was more of an elite job but no one lasted without the eye and the legendary pushy reputation that photographers have earned.

PHOTOGRAPHERS MORE THAN PICTURE TAKERS

"You have to remember that photographers are journalists, too. They are not just people who take pictures. To be a good photojournalist, you have to have judgment, an eye for what makes a story, and the ability to see the beginning, middle, and end of any segment you shoot. A good photojournalist needs two things—the eye for pictures and the 'nose' to see what will make a good story."

Alvarez was also a self-starter, a definite prerequisite, he says. "No one is going to tell you what to shoot. That's up to you. You're on your own." Unfortunately, just as Alvarez was getting into high gear as a photojournalist, the accident happened, which limited his ability to carry a camera. And with the accident his photography career went down the drain. At the time, Alvarez thought his 18 years of toil were wasted and gone. But, in reality, the injury—and the connections he had made—opened a door that enabled the former photojournalist to apply his talents in an area he never thought possible. Alvarez's "second career" is an example of how vitally important it is to network and learn more than one skill.

Les Rose always seemed to have photojournalist talent, even as early as the fifth grade when he edited the school newspaper, and then in the 7th when he took his first pictures for the publication. Rose is the epitome of another characteristic that many photojournalists display—a daring and bravado that refuses to let them quit. While others may be discouraged by a closed gate or door, Rose has never let barriers get in the way. "Frankly," he says, "photographers have to be a bit pushy."

From the time he decided on carrying a camera for a career, Rose had a plan in mind and knew exactly how he was going to climb the ladder. It was simple. "Just go from one market to another. Build your reputation. Start in smaller markets and then shoot for the big ones." In many ways, Rose was thinking like a corporate employee—climb the ladder, one rung at a time. He started at the same station that hired him as an intern, WFLA-TV in Florida. The wages were not much better than an intern's either, $5 an hour (versus the $3.50 an hour he made as an intern).

WFLA was not a giant station or market, but from Rose's perspective that offered an advantage. "Start in a major market without any on-the-job (camera) training and you might goof up your career for good. There are many more demands in a major metro market for photographers, and the competition is stiffer, too. Put a rookie photojournalist up against a pro in a big market, and he'll die."

HOW TO START IN A SMALL MARKET

Rose knew better. He was smart and aggressive. By starting in a small market, he was able to "cover as many as three wraps or packages (stories) a day." A wrap entails writing, the narration of the story, the sound (controlling and putting in), the interviews, and, of course, pictures. Rose remembers the cameras, too. "They were heavy when I first got into the business, and you carried both sound and camera. You could be looking at 30 pounds or more on one shoulder . . . the cameras are lighter today—you're looking at 27 pounds."

Rose was always eyeing the next market up and promoting his talents. "You have to if you hope to get beyond a small market." He went to Central America where he shot drug stories and to make the most out of the segment, he would send a postcard to editors in larger (or major metropolitan) markets from his location to show them he was busy.

But the larger markets did not fall in immediately. For the first four or five years, he continued to work in smaller markets for low pay. He never gave up. "It burns inside of you. You're creativity on the run," he says thoughtfully, trying to explain the role of the photojournalist who has the "calling." When he covered Hurricane Ineki, he was convinced him that "photojournalists had one of the best jobs on earth."

Rose's recognition, however—the 17 Emmy nominations and five wins along with a spot on one of the leading stations in the country—was still to come. Whatever success he has had, however, he credits to his starting (and learning) at stations in smaller markets.

MILLER'S *STAR WARS* PROMOTION

Generating press coverage and stories for clients is what Craig Miller seemed destined for in the entertainment field. The work he had done for George Lucas in publicizing *Star Wars* had established him as one of the leading promotion and PR people in the industry.

"At the time," says Miller, "PR was looked upon as a great opportunity for promoting films. It was cheaper than advertising and had more credibility because it was the media writing or talking about the client, and not the studio through an advertisement."

The challenge of the business, says Miller, was coming up with "different ways of doing things." You needed imagination, and you had to be able to write press releases that "would entice an editor to write a story." Miller also did a lot of promotion-related travel for *Star Wars*. He visited conventions and science fiction clubs. "It was a grass-roots promotion program, and I did the same for a lot of other films that I promoted after the Lucas venture."

Miller says he used "common sense" in his promotion career. For instance, he did his own market research. If he was promoting a science fiction film, he would go to a major newsstand and pluck out all the science fiction publications. From there, he would turn to the mastheads, find the editors, telephone numbers and addresses, and add them to his list. When he did press releases, he sent them to those publications. Miller, who also promoted *American Graffitti*, handled it in a manner similar to *Star Wars*. Instead of science fiction publications, he went to hot rod and automobile publications. As a result, *Graffitti* became an enormous hit.

Promotion, however, was not Miller's destiny. Even though it remains one of the most important jobs in the industry, those choosing it should be aware that it has changed. "It takes a different person." Part of the changes, according to Miller, is that some of the filmmakers feel they are above publicity, and they no longer want to take the time for it.

How Studio Executives Have Changed

"People running the studios have changed, too," he says. "Instead of creative executives, there are a great many lawyers, accountants, and MBAs. They want to know things like 'how many impressions do they get for a dollar that is spent.' Publicity and promotion cannot be measured that way. You are looking at a process that generates positive word-of-mouth, newspaper, and magazine coverage, stories on television and interviews. Those areas cannot be calculated insofar as impressions vs. dollars spent."

Today, publicity and promotion has taken on a new twist. When a well-known personality stars in a motion picture or on a television series, the publicity company will often oblige the media by setting up interviews. But, in many cases, the interviews have changed. With big name stars, the PR firm frequently has "copy approval." That is, the story is approved by the agency (and star) before it goes to print or is aired.

PR firms can drive a hard bargain with the media. If they have access to a well-known personality, that is, one that the media (magazine, newspaper, television show, etc.) wants to reach, the terms of the interview are frequently dictated by the public relations firm. What can and cannot be asked. What can be printed. The pictures that can and cannot be used. And, some firms will only supply a major star for an interview if the magazine (or whatever media outlet is involved) agrees to do another personality (often one that is not a star) immediately afterwards.

On the other side of the fence, the media—which always used to listen to pitches from promotion and PR people—now screen calls via voice mail. In the "old days," the salesmanship of an individual PR man or woman could oftentimes sway an editor, but that opportunity is rarely there anymore.

Miller saw the changes coming long ago when "one famous director I was handling on behalf of a newly released picture told me that what I wanted to do sounded like a stunt. It was! If we can't do things like that, things that will pay off in more people seeing a motion picture, play, or whatever you are promoting, what's the sense of promoting things?"

That question bothered Miller to the point that he eventually decided to leave the promotion business. Switching occupations for those in non-entertainment enterprises is usually difficult. But, those in entertainment rarely encounter that obstacle because of the diverse experience they have had. This is especially true of PR people. Most have dealt (or represented) everyone from casting directors and producers to writers. They've absorbed and learned many of those skills.

THE PLACE TO DEVELOP SKILLS

Like Craig Miller, Andy Epstein was another entertainment industry talent who developed his skills in the PR field. As was the case with Miller, Epstein decided the occupation was not for him, despite the fact he was able to promote some of the leading entertainment figures in the industry.

"Although there was great opportunity in PR, I never felt at home doing it," he says. "If you like hanging out with rock stars and other personalities, it could be the occupation for you. It wasn't for me, though." Epstein saw himself on the other side of the fence. That is, instead of being someone who tried to sell stories to the media, he wanted to be the person (media) writing and covering those stories.

Once he decided to forego PR and concentrate on the media side of entertainment, his career began to climb rapidly. From freelance *Calendar Magazine* (L.A. *Times*) writer, to PBS reporter, Rona Barrett (*Good Morning, America*) writer, to *Entertainment Tonight,* the E Channel, and finally to Fox to head *Entertainment Daily Journal* (EDJ), a daily show that specialized in covering news of the entertainment industry.

Epstein's climb illustrates what frequently happens. There is no track to follow, but once you begin to establish a track record, doors open. Epstein became noted for his ability to dig out hard hitting news about entertainment.

Epstein's challenge is markedly different from someone who is putting together an entertainment-oriented interview show, such as Jay Leno or David Letterman. Leno and Letterman count on well-known stars to draw in viewers. News magazine shows, however, rely on scoops, inside stories, and the like to attract viewers. Finding these stories takes investigative or bulldog skills. You have to be willing to dig and ask questions, and dig even more. The competition is intense because the airwaves are filled with "entertainment tonight" type broadcasts. Consequently, anyone who aims for a career in the area has to not only know the industry, but where they can find the good stories, the sources, and the people who have the best tips and inside information.

Years ago, when the prime media was print, celebrity news appeared mainly in the columns of writers such as Walter Winchell, Hedda Hopper, and Louella Parsons. The public relations' and promotion people would concentrate on trying to "plant" (or give) the best news they had (about their clients) to one of these well-known "gossip" columnists. But, once media expanded and television became the place to break news, the business changed. PR people not only have to dig up news stories, but those stories have to have visual components as well.

BECOMING A DUAL EMMY WINNER

A dual Emmy Award winner who started at the bottom and came up the hard (and traditional) way in the business is Chuck Bowman. Bowman, who did everything from being a page at NBC to working for minimum wage at a Kansas radio station, is into his "sixth" career in the business. None of these careers have followed a straight line or a direct path. Bowman came up like many others before him (messenger/page), learning as much as he could along the way.

"If you are going to get into this business," says Bowman, "there are many different paths to follow. The simple one is to dive right in. Chances are your first job will be an internship or messenger." Bowman went through the same experience that Rose had—he started and learned in a small market. "Smaller markets are where you are more likely to find an opportunity, opening and the chance to do more than one thing." Bowman used the audition tape he had cut at NBC (when he was a page) to land a job in the midwest, and from there he was off and running, changing jobs frequently and moving to a better opportunity whenever the chance arose.

He worked at numerous radio and television stations in the midwest and did everything from reading commercials and announcing to the weekend weather, but his major move came when he was in the midwest working at a Tulsa television station. The Tulsa job was one in a long line of announcing-type positions he had landed as the result of the initial NBC tape he had done, and it followed Bowman's philosophy—"this is a building and learning business. You start out knowing little, maybe doing page duties like I did, but if you work hard, you eventually build your knowledge. There is no set path, though. A friend of mine entered the business the same time I did (about 30 years ago). His first job was as a summer relief cameraman. Interestingly, he's still working at the same station he started at."

Bowman has worked for no less than a dozen or so different stations, not counting the numerous production companies that have also hired him for his talents. "I think," he says, "it's a good example of the unpredictableness of the business. You never know where you are going to wind up. You may start with an idea in mind, but circumstances enter in and change you and the direction you're heading."

Where Bowman was heading changed rapidly one November day. While still in Tulsa, at the local television station, he decided to move west during his vacation—and stayed there. Most people with a reasonably stable position in the business would not have made such a risky move. But Bowman left a promising Tulsa television job without hesitation. Why? "I guess if I have to answer that I would say you first have to be passionate about what you want to do. I was. You also have to believe in yourself, think positive, and stick to it. Things don't just pop into your lap in this business. Certainly, you have to be in the right place, but being in that place will not help if you don't have the background, training, and experience."

Moving West was one of the best moves he could have made. He had the experience, and it wasn't long before he landed a job at a local Los Angeles station as producer of the evening sports show. From there he went to the news and in his spare time he began to do some television acting. "I did about 20 to 30 television shows, but my dream was to be a motion picture actor. I began to think about it. After all, I was in my thirties, which is getting old for someone to break into motion pictures. I had to make some choices." That choice was undoubtedly the right one because it not only established Bowman as one of the industry's bright young producers, but it also opened the doors for him to make a key change and move into other entertainment positions.

Why Some Fear Change

Casey Kasem knows about choices and changes, too. One choice he made dramatically altered his professional career. Many disk jockeys and commercial announcers are afraid to make changes—for a good reason. They may have established a reputation as a good announcer and change could destroy the audience and their following. It is difficult to keep an open mind when you have been successful with one approach and, suddenly, someone asks you to try something new.

Casey says anyone pursuing the voice-over or announcing field should not be afraid to alter their style. "Unfortunately," he says, "many disk jockeys are afraid to make changes at the suggestion of the station manager or program director, especially if things have been going well."

For Casey, the suggestion to change came at a time when he was young and flexible. "Frankly, I didn't know it all . . . and I knew I should be willing to listen to good advice from a veteran. Even today, I don't feel I know it all and I'm willing to listen. In fact, any performer should be willing to listen to advice. Realistically, none of us ever have everything mastered."

The problem performers frequently run into is that few people will ever tell them that they can do it better or that they can improve. The more successful a person gets, the more those around him or her are loathe to criticize. They don't want to "fall out of favor." Casey could have been one of those surrounded by "yes" men, but one of his attributes—and a reason for his continued success—is that he has always looked for ways to improve his performance. "I know it is possible to do it better, and you never know when someone's advice will spark an idea and a way to improve."

"Sometimes it is more important to listen when you are on top." Casey was close to the top when he arrived on the West Coast fresh from Detroit, where he had established a reputation as an excellent voice-over announcer as well as a colorful radio actor and personality.

Try Not to Waste Words

In a three-hour show, "I would use as many as 100 canned voices. I tried not to waste words or go off on tangents but say interesting things relevant to the commercials, music, promos, and so on. It often took me as much as eight hours to write the show."

Casey's show was a winner. It was rated number one in San Francisco, but the station manager approached him one day and said to "change it." The manager wanted him to talk to the audience about the artists and their music, as they used to do in the 1940s on radio. "I hadn't the slightest idea what I was going to say, but I accepted the challenge with a positive attitude."

As luck would have it, Casey—who was trying to live up to the manager's edict—found a copy of *Who's Who in Music*, the 1962 edition. It immediately gave him an idea. "That day I began the teaser-biography format which became today's version of *American Top* 40. There is nothing more entertaining than a good story. And there is no better way to keep an audience interested than through a fascinating story."

Aside from teaching Casey the value of a story, it also taught the popular announcer an important lesson, one that he feels is an excellent guideline for anyone breaking into the business. "Remember," he says, "as much as you may love what you are doing, don't think the audience loves it as much as you do. If you have to head in a new direction, make up your mind to do it better than anyone else ever has. If I hadn't accepted the change but had stuck to my old image, I would have limited my appeal and would not be where I am today."

BLINDED BY GLITZ AND GLAMOUR

Jeff Olds could have solved some of his initial problems if he had the benefit of Kasem's advice when he entered the business. Olds says, "I was driven, but—like a lot of people when they get into this business—I did not know exactly what I wanted to do. Sometimes you're blinded by the glitz and glamour, and that can be a real detriment. You've got to try and stay objective, evaluate your skills, and determine if you are doing the thing that is best for you."

Olds changed his career direction when he got involved doing the promotion work for a picture. "It starred Elvira and I was fascinated with it. From that moment on I decided I wanted to do something that involved more production and less promotion."

But, do you give up a job where you are making $800 a week plus commission as a promoter, for a $6 an hour job as a production assistant (PA)? Olds did and, within a year, he had moved up to associate producer. "The associate producer (AP) has a little more responsibility than the PA. Instead of getting coffee and donuts, they usually are out getting film permits and organizing shootings."

Olds says as an AP "you find out that production is not as glamorous as you may think. You are suddenly made aware of details and how important they are. Forget to get a permit and you can shut down production or cost it hundreds of thousands of dollars. The job was much more meticulous than I thought, and you discover that the production may not get done without the stars, but it won't get done without the lowest person on the totem pole, either."

Olds moved up the ladder quickly because he displayed another critical characteristic: "I was determined that whatever job I was given—PA or whatever—I would do better than anyone had before me. I leapfrogged ahead of others, because I never complained about the hours nor refused a request. People don't realize it, but networking and relationships are just as important in the business as talent and creativity."

THE UNDEREXPERIENCED NIGHTMARE

Olds established himself as a go-getter and someone who could get anything done. When there was a need for an associate producer on a documentary that was being filmed in Russia, Olds jumped at it. He landed the position, too, thanks to the contacts and networking he had done for the previous year.

"For me," he recalls, "it was a big jump. I thought I was on my way to even bigger and better things. But I discovered something. I was underexperienced and it turned into the biggest nightmare of my life. I was over my head. The producer hated me because I could not perform." But, Olds survived. "Even though it was tough and I didn't know what I was doing, I worked my tail off and learned while I was doing. Eventually the producer wound up offering me another position. I turned it down. In this business if you don't get along with someone, it does not pay to continue working with them."

In that way, Olds says, entertainment is similar to the corporate world. If a CEO ends up with a chief financial officer he does not like, the CFO may stay—but not for long. Olds could see his fate. "Don't go where you are not wanted," he advises.

Instead, Olds went to work on a new game show for Fox (*Studs*). "They had trouble getting contestants and I volunteered to find some. I worked for commission and it paid off." In some positions, production companies will offer compensation based upon results, such as a commission for every viable contestant. Although many ambitious entertainment workers do not view a commission as desirable as salary, it is often the only way to prove yourself and move up the ladder. Production companies do not want to spend money needlessly and many believe that if there are enough candidates out there, they need not come up with a salary. Commission will suffice.

Olds went to every nightclub in town and brought in contestants from each. As a result, they offered Olds the talent coordinator position. "That was my opportunity," he recalls, "to become a permanent member of the show."

KEY ELEMENT IN GAME SHOWS

"The key thing on any game show is the contestants. They have to have the right personality and say the right things. I had dealt with enough people so I had insight into what type of contestant would be good and which ones would not." Olds was given the job of interviewing and screening the contestants and finding those who could "keep the crowd going" and the show interesting.

Partially because of the effort Olds put into it, *Studs* became a hit and Olds was introduced to Brian Graden, vice president of Fox. Graden saw the potential in the production—and Olds. He wanted the outgoing talent coordinator to do more local promotions with the show. That is, travel across the country and stage events that would call attention to the weekly interview show.

Olds did. The creative, former law student began a whirlwind promotion campaign where he staged and held a contest in twenty different cities and searched for the "biggest local stud." It was a natural, and not only brought the show national attention, but raised Olds' profile in the eyes of the Fox executives. Eventually, he became director of national promotion as well as the show's talent coordinator.

"Brian had faith in me and knew if he gave me something to do, I would do it." That's a critical attribute in the business. In entertainment—as in business—people want to be able to rely upon you. The ability to self-start is a must. As Olds' reliability and reputation spread, his climb up the ladder accelerated. The executives at Fox turned to him whenever there was a difficult assignment, especially if it involved promotion.

"But, I was too brash for my own good," Olds recalls, "and I wanted to be a producer. I had seen people all around me getting stuck in one position and I was determined it was not going to happen to me. I was determined to be a producer, and when they offered me something else I turned it down. Before long I had turned down everything they offered, in hopes of landing the producing position. But, I didn't get it and the next thing I knew I was out on the street, going from $1,000 a week to nothing."

An Attribute You Must Have in the Business

That event taught Olds a lesson: "You have to have patience in this business. You might have all the talent in the world, but there are other people around who have the same attributes. I found that everyone is replaceable. The next person may not be as good, but they can still replace you. It's good to think positive, but don't let it dominate your thoughts and attitude."

Unfortunately, in Olds' case it did and within a week he found himself going from a promising career to a job as a waiter in a Mexican restaurant for minimum wage. Still, Olds had learned a lesson. It would not be long before the aggressive young producer candidate would find himself back behind the scenes.

Olds wasn't the only person in the business who learned how quickly you could go up—and down. Jerad Grimes got a first-hand lesson, too. Grimes, was a runner who was making $400 a week (plus mileage) when his opportunity came along with another series, the *Dating Game*. Grimes heard that one of the production assistants was quitting and he applied for the position. ("That's another advantage in being behind the scenes," he says, "you hear about things before they get outside the studio and you can take advantage of the opportunity—if there is one.")

Grimes was offered the job, and he took it despite the fact it was for less money than he earned as a runner. "It was the smart thing to do, regardless of the pay." PAs can end up doing a variety of oddball duties, but it can pay off. In this case, Grimes kept a database of all the contestants. "I did it for four months, and although it was not the most exciting job, it brought me close to the producers. I got to know them and they knew me."

The producers liked what they saw and, as was the case with Olds, they began to give him more responsibilities. They even let him produce the last two shows of the season, and he was sure that the next season he would come back as a producer. But, as is the case with many businesses, nothing is guaranteed in entertainment. Columbia, the studio that was responsible for the show, changed format and, instead of producing shows, Grimes was laid off.

IMPORTANCE OF CONTACTS AND EXPERIENCE

Columbia did not believe he had the necessary background, and they were not going to take the chance regardless of how ambitious he was. Despite the disappointment, Grimes was sold on the creative end of the business. "There's nothing like it."

Thanks to his contacts, he was able to obtain a position with the *Newlywed Game*, the sister show of the *Dating Game*. The producers of the show, anxious for fresh ideas, held a contest among those behind-the-scenes who were working on it. Grimes' ideas won . . . "everyone knew I was destined for more than running errands . . . the contest proved it, and I was determined." But, it would be months before Grimes finally found his niche.

Tom Sanders was one of those who found a specialized niche, and unlike Grimes and many others, there was little competition. Sanders competed with only four other flying cinematographers in the industry. There have always been photographers who can parachute out of airplanes and shoot, but Sanders brought a new dimension to the trade. He jumped like the others but was able to shoot stills, video, or film—all at the same time. "There are many jobs in the industry that are similar, but if you can put a new twist to something; something that will give the producers and/or client more than they bargained for, than you may have found a real opportunity." Sanders did. On a good day, the free-fall cinematographer will make $2,000 to $3,000 per jump, but it is not easy.

"Not many people feel comfortable soaring through the sky at 120 to 220 mph, with a camera on your helmet. I didn't just suddenly jump out of an airplane and start shooting. It took me a long time to master shooting with three cameras."

Surprisingly, he only jumps about five days out of the month. The rest of the time "I am working putting together proposals for jobs or editing film. I sell a lot of stock footage to libraries and stock photo houses. Much of it is used for adventure films. You can make anywhere from $30 to $1,000 a shot, depending upon how good it is, but typically I earn about $100 a shot. I sell a lot of my work to television shows, but that does not just happen. I have to get out there and knock on doors.

THE DIFFERENCE BETWEEN FILM AND VIDEO

"Motion picture clients call me because I am a cinematographer, which is a lot different than a videographer, or someone who just shoots video. There is a big difference between film and video shooting."

When Sanders shoots video, he can market it only to those who want video, such as *Hard Copy*, *Dateline*, 20/20. "But people who want film want more than just aerial shots. They want to use it for motion pictures." And Sanders has marketed many of his film takes to motion picture production companies. Recently he shot *Drop Zone* with Wesley Snipes, *Point Break*, with Patrick Swayze, and *Terminal Velocity*, with Charlie Sheen.

But Sanders has shot much more than footage for films. There was the opening ceremonies at the Seoul, Olympics and jumping into the Games on opening night. Daring? Of course, but that word can describe most of those who have been successful in the business, whether they jump out of airplanes or not.

Daring is an apt description for Bob Schulenberg, illustrator, animator, producer, and an extraordinary, behind-the-scenes talent. Name it, and Schulenberg has probably done it.

He also has words of advice on breaking in—and staying in—the industry. Schulenberg is one of those who believes it is important to find a mentor or become a protege. Schulenberg did that early on in his career. He was barely out of his teens, when he met Al Nickel, head of Western Costume. Nickel gave Schulenberg his first break with a freelance design job. He also opened the doors so that Schulenberg was not only able to show his artistic ability to clients, but he introduced the young designer to people like Edith Head, a costume designer who had won numerous Oscars.

After working for Nickel for a short time, Schulenberg was hired (at the ripe old age of 22) to head up Berman's, a London costumer who was opening a storefront in Los Angeles.

With Berman's he did everything from costuming for Minsky's burlesque to the Lido de Paris. "In this business, it is important to get a variety of experiences. Develop and show your creativity. I learned about spectacle and how to put together spectacular effects and designs."

Movies Were Directionless

Despite his success, Schulenberg's efforts to get into the motion picture field were stymied. "Frankly," he recalls, "at that time movies were directionless. They were scrambling to stay in business, and the big blockbuster films we are familiar with today were nonexistent." Traditional animation was dying and technology had not yet taken hold of the industry. In fact, instead of thriving, motion picture studios were auctioning off their back lots and turning them into real estate developments. "It was not the best time to try and break into the business." Today the climate is much more favorable.

With the obstacles he faced, Schulenberg decided to leave Los Angeles and go to New York. Nickel told him that despite his design capabilities he would be better off going to Manhattan where he might find work as an advertising illustrator—and not a costume designer—because opportunities were more plentiful and promising. Schulenberg was realistic. "You have to be in this business. You need to work hard, but if there is no opportunity, if no one is making films, you are not going to find work."

Schulenberg went to New York, put together his portfolio and showed it to the father of a good friend, who happened to own an advertising agency. "He offered me a job as an art director in his agency. That's where I learned a great deal."

What? "People get jobs by meeting people." He also theorized there was a radical difference between how things were done on the East and West Coast. In New York if someone draws well, they have an excellent chance of becoming a freelance illustrator. "As an art director of the agency," recalls Schulenberg, "I gave a job to a young illustrator named Andy Warhol." That would not, says Schulenberg, have happened in Los Angeles, because there are not an abundance of opportunities for freelancers.

Schulenberg says there is a definite difference between the coast and the opportunities each present. "In L.A. it is much easier to be anonymous because it is so big geographically. My first night in New York, I met a young lady who was a friend of someone I knew in L.A. She had won a talent contest in Greenwich Village and the prize was an audition in a well-known New York club. She opened in the club and there were several syndicated columnists in the audience. They made her—Barbra Streisand— nationally known. It was a big lesson for me. You would never have seen that happen in L.A., because there isn't a club in L.A. that anyone cares enough about. Appear in a club in L.A., and you may never break through."

RULES FOR ENTERTAINMENT

Schulenberg has devised some rules that he recommends strongly. "A mistake a lot of artists and illustrators make— whether they are trying to get in the entertainment field or some other avenue—is they tend to be scattered." By that, Schulenberg means that artists/illustrators and animators try to show "too much" when they go in for a job. They run the gamut, and hope by showing many different sides to their ability, they will land a job. Not true, says Schulenberg.

"When you are competing for something—a job or whatever—be focused. Do not show all the things you can do. In being general and broad you don't grab anyone's attention. Concentrate on one thing, one talent. That's what makes an impression."

Your name and reputation mean everything, too. Once, he designed an advertisement in Andy Warhol style for the back page of *The New York Times*. His fee—$150. Warhol's would have been $3,000. Schulenberg looked at his fee and thought about Warhol's compensation. That's all it took. He began to focus on one particular style in hopes of attracting attention and more income.

Schulenberg's talent stood out when he created illustrations that might have been used in magazines published in the 1920s. The style began to generate work and notoriety for him. Just when he thought he had hit a winning combination, things changed again. General interest magazines began to die, and niche magazines became the rage. The mass market magazine were replaced by shows like *Today* and *Good Morning, America*.

Illustration was changing, too. With the demise of magazines there was less of a market for an art director and illustrator. Schulenberg decided to go back to the West Coast, but not before three of his illustrations were used for *Time* magazine covers. The advertising trades wrote glowingly of his accomplishments, but that did not pay the bills. Still, Schulenberg returned to Los Angeles and unbeknownst to him, his career in motion pictures was about to flourish to such an extent that even Jim Carey would take note of it.

NEW BREED OF MANAGERS

While Schulenberg was trying to make his mark as an illustrator/artist, Paul Addis was becoming one of the first in a new breed of personal managers. Addis' rise to head of Ambitious Entertainment, a personal management company, is one that is symptomatic of the young agents and managers who are entering the business.

Addis did not have any idea of becoming a manager, but he turned into one of the best in the business. When he was 18 years of age, he moved to Los Angeles from Chicago, and worked as a singer/songwriter at night, opened up a retail music store during the day and sold guitars and synthesizers. His entry into the management field was, as he puts it, "quite unusual."

Numerous musicians were attracted to his store, and one day a guitar player (Oingo Boingo) came in and told Addis that his group had been approached by a manager who would handle them for 40 percent. Without hesitating, Addis said he would do it for 15 percent—and within minutes he had his first act.

What's it take to be a good manager? "It is," he says, "a thankless job. But you have to remember, you are negotiating for people who do not like to haggle about money. You do. A good manager not only negotiates but he watches out for his client's money, their tours, the box office sales, record sales, and tours."

Addis, who has negotiated many record deals for his clients (Caldera with Capitol, for instance) says that the best prerequisite for a personal manager is "good business sense" and being able "to deal with people. I was in sales (retail) since I was 15 years of age, and knew how to relate to customers. Record labels, club owners—they are the same as the customers I dealt with at the retail level. You are not dealing for yourself, but a client. You are not selling (retail) for yourself, but the store owner."

Addis views the role of a manager as much more than someone who negotiates fees, dates, and contracts. That may have been the modus operandi years ago, but today's manager is more diversified. Addis sees two key differences between the old time manager, and the contemporary person who guides an artist's career.

Niche Management Needed

"First, if you are going to be a success, you need to find a niche. You can't manage all different kinds of people, because you can't possibly know the ins and outs of performers ranging from actors and actresses to choreographers, musicians, and commercial announcers. There are literally dozens of careers, and a manager does best by focusing on a limited number. The business—like many in other industries—has become a specialty. You can no longer be all things to all performers. Pick a couple on concentrate on them."

That's what Tony Selznick has done. Selznick is an agent and, in contrast to agents who represented artists years ago, he concentrates on two categories of performers—dancers and choreographers. "The business is changed." Managers need to look for other opportunities. They should be negotiating commercial deals for clients. "If you just sit back and wait for offers, it will not happen. A good manager has to make things happen. They've got to be salespeople. They should also be focusing on one aspect or niche. Don't try to manage all kinds of people in different entertainment areas. Focus on just two or three."

That's what Addis does. "I looked for the need and the opportunity." For instance, why go into the management of music personalities when there are literally hundreds around. "Try something with some synergy . . . I picked three categories because they all related to one another—commercial directors, photographers, and designers."

Commercial companies need directors who, in turn, hire photographers and designers for the film. Addis has also chosen these three because he can show a company how they can film a commercial (using his three talents) and save money at the same time. "Normally, if you are a commercial director, a company may sign you for a year to work on a commercial. That company, however, is obligated to pay a hefty salary plus benefits.

With our setup they can hire a quality commercial director, pay them a day rate and move on."

HONING IN ON COMMERCIALS

Both Selznick and Addis believe that specialization and "boutique" personal managers and agents are rapidly becoming one of the most promising ventures in the entertainment field. They also see that handling talent opens the door to an entirely new career for agents and managers—production.

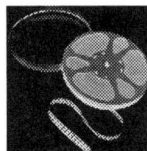

CHAPTER FOUR

Getting to the Top—Some of the Jobs That Get You There and What You Actually Do

Breaking into the business and climbing the ladder is one thing, but getting to the top and earning a six- or seven-figure income is quite another. Those who do it, usually find a different approach, unique niche, or they are in on the ground floor of a new venture.

Take Don Graham. In 1998, he had one of his best years ever from a financial standpoint. Why? Because Graham has stayed up-to-date with radio. When he first broke in, stations played music strictly for entertainment, and one station frequently played a variety of different kinds of music. Today, there is a different format for every kind of music—one station plays rap, another hip hop, others country, adult, adult contemporary, and so on. Specialties galore. No longer does one person cover radio stations with varying formats.

Graham knows you cannot take a hip hop record to an adult contemporary station, and vice versa. He is also aware that he has a better rapport and understands some formats better than others, and the ones he comprehends, he sticks with. Consequently, when Graham takes a record to a station, it usually gets played.

After more than 30 years in the business, Graham is proof that good promotion men never go out of style. Graham's advice to those who want to enter promotion or, for that matter, any other entertainment occupation: "Keep your ears to the ground. Listen to what's happening, because this business, more than any other, changes, and it can do so rapidly."

Graham, admittedly, never planned his career. "It just happened." But, he was in the right place at the right time, and he knew the business. Graham is also a pioneer and innovator. He seldom does things the traditional, established way. That's one reason he has done so well. He thinks originally. Graham has been in on the ground floor of two ventures, and then—when most figured that the radio promoters were heading for extinction—he did it again. That is, he put a new twist on an old approach and became an enormous success, once again.

CAN CHOOSE ANY FORMAT

Graham's first big hit in the entertainment/promotion field occurred shortly after he found his way into the record business, where he earned $200 a month setting up top 40 record racks in retail stores around San Francisco. From there, Graham became a promotion man for Warner Bros., then an independent promotion man handling a variety of labels, then national promotion director for A&M Records, and finally a niche promotion specialist where he concentrates on getting airplay and sales for adult standards, which used to be called easy listening or nostalgia records.

Regardless of what radio format a promotion person wants to work, they can. It only takes a few qualifications, according to Graham—"hard work, long hours, and an honest ear." That is, don't go after airplay if you believe the record your touting is a stiff. Remember, too, record promotion is no different than sales and in order to be an effective salesperson you have to "have a good product and understand the customer's (radio station and consumer) needs."

An indication of how wide open the field is comes from Graham, who remembers when he went to work for Warners. The opportunity dropped in his lap while he was working in the back of the warehouse that had been set up to house top 40 stock. He was visited by a representative from Warner Bros. Pictures (WB), who told Graham that Warners was going into the record business and they needed him to handle promotion in the Bay Area. They wanted someone who knew all the Bay Area disk jockeys and program directors—and the logical choice was Graham. There was only one problem, Graham had never dealt with disk jockeys, but because of the offer from WB, he was more than willing to try. Despite the fact he had never taken a record to a station for airplay, Warners was under the impression that his relationships were such that he would be the most productive radio promotion man in the country. He took the challenge.

Graham's approach was, if anything, creative. "I did," he recalls, "what anyone would do if they were looking for a station. I went to the telephone book, found the Yellow Pages where the radio stations were listed, tore out the page, and started calling on every one of them. Then, I went to the station, introduced myself, told them I was representing Warners, and asked what day they heard new records." It was that simple and Graham was in business. "When you think about it," recalls Graham, "it was no more than common sense.

Sometimes we forget how important that is in this—and every—business."

Graham had an iron-clad rule that he credits with helping his business grow. "Never try to sell anything you don't believe in." If he wouldn't play it, he did not expect the station to, either. As a result, his reputation began to grow. Within a few months, he was known to every station manager and program director. He also had some of the hottest product in the market (Ed Kookie Byrnes' "Kookie, Kookie, Lend Me Your Comb").

Does Not Require Special Skills

"It did not," he recalls, "take a lot of intelligence. I think anyone could do the same thing. What it did take, of course, is good product and genuine enthusiasm. I can't stress that enough. People recognize sincerity—and insincerity."

Graham eventually left Warners and opened his own independent promotion company. "Creating your own enterprise is not easy. I was both a promoter and salesman, and ran the operation out of a warehouse." Eighteen-hour days were commonplace, and Graham would post a sign on the door that said, "Gone to the Radio Station." Everyone understood.

Graham's reputation and his credibility soared. He took a fledgling enterprise—A&M Records—and helped make it one of the major new independent labels. In fact, it was his enormous success with "The Lonely Bull" and A&M that shot him into the big time.

In the industry, however, Graham is equally as well known for the impact he had on another phase of the record industry—distribution. Up until "Lonely Bull," wholesalers would come to Graham, or any record distributor, purchase records on credit, and return whatever didn't sell without ever paying the full bill. They had the best of both worlds. They could always wait to see which records became hits before they purchased stock, and they seldom had to put out any money.

Great for the wholesalers, but frustrating and cash draining for the labels. In many cases, start-up labels would go into bankruptcy because they never received payment.

New Muscle Developed

But, "Lonely Bull" gave Graham's sales arm new muscle. The wholesalers (that is, the people who supplied retailers with product) desperately needed "Lonely Bull" because of demand. Consumers were deluging the local record stores with requests, and the retailers knew if they did not comply, those customers would be going elsewhere for the "Lonely Bull" as well as all their other purchases. Customers pressured and threatened wholesalers and distributors. However, no one had stock because Graham controlled the distribution. Graham was willing to supply the record, but "before I did they had to pay for it. No one had ever forced them to do that. A&M was a new label, they needed the money and I saw the demand as a way to get it." Graham also realized something else. If A&M did not get some cash flow, they would not be in business long, and he would be out one promising client.

He had seen too many other start-up labels come up with hit records, and then go broke because wholesalers held back payment. Big name retailers were notorious for squeezing small labels in hopes they would go bankrupt, thus eliminating the need for the wholesaler to ever pay. Although it did not happen to A&M, it did to others. The industry is noted for the start-up labels tht have a hit and are squeezed into bankruptcy by slow-paying retailers and distributors.

But thanks to Graham, with "Lonely Bull" every wholesaler and distributor came through with money—up front. "I got the checks to Jerry (Jerry Moss, one of A&M's owners), he deposited them, and got the money to Monarch, the record-pressing plant, that produced the records almost overnight. The next day I went to the airport with a trailer and picked up 25,000 records and delivered them. By running the operation on a tight, cash basis we were able to establish the label and put A&M in business."

A&M was impressed, and they brought Graham to Los Angeles to handle their national radio promotion. "Believe it or not," he says, "I did the same thing nationally as I did in San Francisco. For the next five years, I traveled to every major city with 'Lonely Bull' and other product we had, and in each market I went to the Yellow Pages, tore out the radio station listings, and made personal calls on each."

Sophisticated? "You don't need to be a brain surgeon to make it in this business," he laughs. "Can you think of a better way to make money? If you have something that everyone wants, you are in the driver's seat."

LEVERAGE OVER TABLOIDS

That philosophy is still true today. If you have any commodity that someone wants, you can usually get what you want. Hollywood and New York publicists, who represent major film, stage, and television stars—stars who are in demand by the public—have a similar leverage with the media. Look at the covers of such magazines as *People*. They always feature a well-known celebrity or personality, because that's what the audience (consumers) want. Motion pictures utilize well-known stars for the same reason. They have to cater to the moviegoer, just as television has to cater to the viewer. Entertainment companies must provide audiences with what they (the consumers) want. If they did not, they would not be in business long. Graham gives this advice to anyone entering the business— "don't try and dictate to the consumer. Give them what they want and you can be successful."

Today, promoters like Graham still knock on radio station doors, but the process has changed. Aside from niche marketing, record labels, says Graham, "pay market researchers huge fees to put consumers in an auditorium and let them listen and vote on new records. That was exactly what we did before computers, only instead of putting people in an auditorium, we would get the record played. If the listener liked it, they would call the station and ask to have it played again, or they would go to the store and buy a copy. It was infallible market research."

With that approach Graham—who has been at the top of his profession for years—once had three albums in the top 10 at the same time. He was named Promotion Man of the Year by *Billboard Magazine*, and Bill Gavin, one of the most influential publishers (his weekly *Gavin Report* is considered the bible of the industry) has named him National Promotion Man of the Year three different times.

Graham says you don't need sophisticated market research to make it in the business. Human nature has not changed. "There are still opportunities. It all goes back to the music. A bright promotion man can make it big." People enter the business differently. Take Donny Cohen, a bright, honest young music lover who—as Graham would say—loved the music. Donny, started, as so many others did, in the mailroom at Universal, and within five years was one of the top promotion men in the country.

RADIO STATIONS HAVE CHANGED

Although the basics are still the same—the audience has to like the record enough to buy it—the business has changed. Whereas stations used to have meetings on certain days of the week, today you have to know if the record fits a particular format. It is not just a matter of rock, rap, or country. There are "at least 19 or 20 formats," says Graham. "Everyone has a niche, and you have to know which one your record fits. Some stations are wide open. They are up for hearing anything, but for the most part, you need to know who is playing what."

Niche marketing is growing rapidly in entertainment. Everyone is becoming a specialist. Tom Sanders is one of only four (as of this writing) stuntmen who jump out of airplanes and can shoot video, stills, and film. Most stuntmen/cameraman shoot only one. Agent Tony Selznick represents only choreographers, and Paul Addis is a personal manager who handles only directors, photography directors, and production designers.

You can learn any of these professions, including promotion, and get to the top as Graham did. The best way? Graham says, "Go to work for an independent distributor. They have, maybe 40 to 60 different lines or labels. You can listen to new releases and find something that makes you crazy.

"Go to the boss, convince him that this is your niche, a format you love, and one in which you can break a record. If I had a guy working for me who was that anxious, I would give him a shot. Chances are you can get one and find your opportunity and niche."

HOW TO COPY SUCCESS

Special effects has become the niche for Brick Price. He had engineering skills which he learned in aerospace, art skills, animation talents, and cinematography ability. He put all those things together and created a company that fascinated Gene Roddenberry to the extent that the *Star Trek* creator hired Price's firm for the popular sci fi television series.

Can others copy Price's success? "Yes," he says, although his background is varied and would not appear to be easily duplicated. Price says there is a way. Someone can actually emulate the set designs, animation techniques, and illustration skills he utilizes. They are complex, but he says "you can learn it. You have to be willing to work your way up, though. If you like this end of the business, you can make it. But plan on starting where everyone else does—as a production assistant. Get used to running and getting the donuts, like everyone else."

Price's 18-year-old son is a donut "fetcher." He began as a production assistant and "he has gotten to know people, and see the skills that are needed. That's one of the keys, meet people and learn." The younger Price wants to position himself for filming travel documentaries, and his father sees no reason the boy will fail—as long as he "has the work ethic and creativity." That's one of the unique aspects of the entertainment business. Nearly everyone starts at the same, similar low level, but after that they branch out and there is no limit.

Price's technique, however, is not the easiest even though it is "learnable. We can do everything from building models—which vary in size in the same scene—and we can shoot them as well. We're not talking about computerization, but actual models.

"It's similar to the way we did the train crash in Union Station. The train was a miniature, and the people were lifesize. By working the camera a certain way, it appeared as if the train went through the wall of the station and all the people scattered for cover at the same time."

The computer helps, but does not completely replace the miniaturization. Still it has a role. "Take *True Lies*," says Price. "We had an airplane that was hung on wires with Arnold Schwarzenegger in the cockpit. In the past, they would have used fine, high tensil wires that were virtually invisible to the camera's eye. But they had an extremely small margin of safety. Today, we can use safer materials and get rid of the wires through the computer. But, we don't build the entire set with computers."

THE BREAK THAT MADE DIFFERENCE

Most who have made it in the business can look back to a particular event or break that provided the impetus for their success. That's particularly true of Richard Alvarez and the back injury that ended his photojournalist career.

Just when it appeared that Alvarez's career was through, he got the break that made the difference. The station was impressed with the news skills he had learned through the years, and slotted him in as special assignment news editor, where he suddenly found himself covering stories from inside the studio instead of out in the field. At first, Alvarez admits, it was difficult getting used to the switch. Then he discovered the trick to becoming a good news editor.

"This is a fast business, but the one thing that remains the same, whether you are talking photojournalism or editing, the key thing is the story. If you're good in this business you can spot one. The best photographers see it before they even point their cameras, and editors must do the same thing." For Alvarez, 18 years of shooting and news coverage paid handsome dividends in the newsroom.

In the newsroom, the producer and reporter usually decide on the story and the editor puts the footage together, mixes the sound and inserts the music. Being a special assignment editor (or for that matter, any editor), however, involves more than just editing and putting music and shots together. The technology is a challenge in itself. "Digital computers are the standard, and you find there is oftentimes resistance on the part of reporters and people in the newsroom when it comes to technology. Most people do not want the system they know well, and rely upon, suddenly replaced." But, says Alvarez, the old, hard-drinking, cigar smoking editor is on the way out. He is being replaced by the person who can put together a story in a half-hour—thanks to technology.

How He Earned His Emmy

Alvarez realized what was happening and when a new computer and digital system (ADID) came in, he was one of the few who volunteered to learn it. "Don't ever think you know it all. We can all learn." Alvarez did, and for it last year he earned an Emmy for an investigative series that dug into the restaurant industry and the unsanitary conditions. The series stirred such a furor in the city (Los Angeles) that the politicians in the community had every eating establishment in Los Angeles rated (A, B, C, D) and the eatery's standing was posted in the window. The coverage the story received was enormous. It (and CBS) were written about in *The Los Angeles Times.*

The experience convinced Alvarez that investigative reporting, both in and out of the entertainment business, was here to stay. But the business is changing. "The old-style reporter is gone. The days of sitting on a story, investigating it, and taking inordinate amounts of time to write it are gone. This is an instant business. Take all the time you want—as long as it is written in 30 minutes. Many of the old ways of doing things still apply, but with all the media out there it has become enormously competitive and we have to do things faster and better."

No longer do photojournalists just shoot film. Ninety-five percent of the shots taken make the air. The editor does not have the time to waste and neither do the journalists. "If it isn't worth airing, don't shoot it."

Even with the technology and innovative equipment, news coverage is still a business that "is learned by doing," Alvarez says. Like other facets of entertainment, it is learned from the ground up, and the runner who goes to get the coffee may one day be the next network news anchor.

Les Rose may not be the next Dan Rather—although he could probably outtalk him—but he is considered one of the finest photojournalists in the country. He climbed to the top thanks to a combination of gifts. A natural eye for the shot, a nose for news and a bulldog personality that refuses to let him give up before he shoots the complete story.

THE PREREQUISITE FOR PHOTOJOURNALISTS?

Stories are legendary about photographers pushing and shoving their way into a party or event. The photojournalists were pointed to as the cause behind the disastrous and fatal automobile crash that took the life of Princess Diana. When celebrities come out, the photojournalists are not far behind. Does it take pushing and shoving to make it in the business?

Rose, who has worked for NBC and CBS as well as numerous independent channels, views successful photojournalists as those who not only know their job, but they understand they are competing with other networks, local channels, cable stations, and other media. "That takes aggressiveness," he says, "but that does not mean pushing and shoving or invading someone's privacy." It also takes someone who believes in themself. When Rose was trying to land a job on one of the network affiliates, he sent out nearly 200 resumes. He kept every rejection letter and mounted a good portion of them on his wall.

He still laughs when he recalls what happened when he sent out 186 letters and resumes in search of a job. From one, he was offered a one-week temporary job with a station in Tampa. The station also supplied him with an extra week's training. After two weeks—one week of training and one week on the job— Rose did not go home. "I kept showing up. I would walk in the newsroom and someone would put me to work. About eight months later, payroll finally caught on. It is that hectic in the newsroom."

Rose looks back on the Tampa experience with fondness. In addition to the week's training, they made him edit everyone else's work for months before they would let him shoot. "You learn the importance of cutaways, holding shots, sequencing. I learned how vital it was to determine whether you want a wide shot or a narrow one. All those things I absorbed by having to edit everyone else's footage." It's a good indicator of what Rose means when he says you never know what you are going to learn and where you are going to learn it. Even veteran photojournalists can learn.

WINS FIVE EMMYS

Rose's daring did not end in Tampa. When he decided to come to the West Coast because of the increased opportunities, he sent footage, letters, and resumes to the editor of the local Los Angeles CBS affiliate. "The reality of the business," he says, "is that if there is an opening in a major market, the editor is going to pluck someone locally. Usually, there is not a shortage of good photojournalists in key markets." Despite that, Rose would not give up. He even telephoned the editor and asked if he would be willing to give Rose 20 minutes if he flew—at his own expense—3,000 miles for the interview. The editor agreed, Rose flew out—and got the job. Daring, audacity, boldness, nerve. Rose has them all—along with five Emmys.

If Les Rose had daring, then Craig Miller had a double dose. Despite the list of prominent clientele, Miller wanted out of promotion. Changing careers is nothing new, but dumping a successful venture for a seemingly, unrelated career does not happen too often.

Miller had a successful PR firm, was well-connected to potential clients, and was on his way to the top of the profession but he wanted to write. Familiar story? The industry is filled with many would-be writers, but Miller was not a would-be. He found that a friend of his was responsible for writing 65 episodes of an animated television series. Miller convinced his friend to let him pen a sample. The friend agreed and the story idea he turned in was strong enough to earn Miller a script assignment. That was Miller's first move toward the top of the ladder, but it would never have happened if the former PR man had not kept networking.

The impact of networking has never been lost on Miller. "None of this would have ever happened if it wasn't for contacts or networking. The chances of walking in and getting someone to let me do a script were nil. You don't get anywhere in this business without other people."

Miller's one episode turned into three, and he went on to write for *The Real Ghostbusters*, a series based on the motion picture. Networking came into play again. Michael Stracvynski, who was the story editor for the series, became creator of *Babylon 5*, and Miller had another opportunity.

Establishing Animation Reputation

Miller's storytelling was not confined to sci fi series. It was in animation that he made his mark and established a reputation. He not only became noted for his animation writing ability, and for the talent he displayed in writing for children on television.

"Writing for animated shows is different, just as writing for children is, too. The difference in animation and regular film is that in live action you can have two people in a room talking. You cannot do that in animation. They can be talking but you have to have things happening. With animation, you have to be and think more visually. It is not a matter of dialog, but rather movement and action."

Another major difference that Miller cites for those pursuing an animated career, is in live action television there is generally what is called a "master scene. Fred walks into the room, George is standing there, and you describe the physical things in the room that are important. In animation, there are no live actors to work with and the only stuff in the room (or scene) is what the writer comes up with . . . in many ways it is harder."

Writing for children is different, too. "For children, you do not need as much depth as you would for *Murphy Brown* or *Home Improvement*. In those shows, there has to be substance, logical flow. But with children the most important elements are that the story has to be targeted and easy to understand. There is little room for sophistication."

For those pondering a career in animation, Miller describes how it is done. The script is written first, then comes the voices and the artists who do the recording. Animation comes last, but it is, of course, critically important. Every shot is called and described by the writer. "The writer has to think out everything, because animation is intensely visual. It is not like live action, where the characters can carry the action."

WHERE WRITER HAS CONTROL

Miller—and many other writers—prefer animation because "the writer has much more control of the material." There are, however, two different animation approaches. One is daytime and the other prime time. Check the *Simpsons* versus a daytime series and the changes become more obvious.

Miller's goal, however, was not just to continue writing animated shows for others. Although the pay scale is good—anywhere from $5,000 to $8,500 for a daytime show, and $15,000 to $17,000 for prime time—the payoff is in creating, owning, and selling your own. So, Miller and a partner took a shot and sold one show concept to ABC, just before Disney took over the network. As often happens in entertainment, when there is a sale or change, everything goes including executives and shows that were under development (i.e., Miller's). But that did not stop Miller.

Miller and his partner soon developed *Pocket Dragon Adventures*, which debuted last year on the BKN Kids Network, which is a syndicated group of stations similar to UPN or WB. The sale, though, is not as easy as it sounds. First, Miller developed the series idea. "The developer," he explains, "is primarily creative. We acquired the rights to an artist's characters, and developed them for the series. We went out as producers and tried to get a company to finance our efforts. BKN did, and gave us the best opportunity to retain control of the show." Thus, Miller and his partner are creators, executive producers, and responsible for the writing. They also approve the voices of the actors.

"Developers," says Miller, "must be writers." They may have created the characters, but they have to be able to write, as well. Miller says he got in the door, once again, because of contacts, networking, and background. Otherwise BKN would never have listened.

"Anyone with experience can probably get in to see at least the lower level development people," says Miller. "In animation, in particular, the doors are open. The more experience, the better the opportunity." Interestingly, not everyone with an animated idea has to be an animator. They may just have an idea, and if the company likes what they hear, they may hire someone to help in the development. But, says Miller, remember this is a business and even though the doors are open, people hire people they believe will deliver the most and the best. You are not," he stresses, "going to see your mother or uncle. You need sample scripts, and art work. This is a job and it is more fun than waiting tables, but it is still a job."

BASICS FOR MOST NEWS SHOWS

Dual Emmy winner Andy Epstein knows what Miller is talking about. He held numerous jobs and, although they were more fun than waiting tables, he was after a more serious news position after earning a reputation in entertainment. Thanks to *Entertainment Daily Journal* (EDJ), Fox's entertainment news show which was wrapped up in a daily journal format, Epstein came to the attention of CBS affiliate, KNXT.

Epstein had shown his news-gathering ability, and his organizational skills as supervising producer of a demanding, daily show that aired nationwide on Fox. Although news is competitive, there are few shows moreso than those that are entertainment oriented. The basics for most local news shows are the same—it's local breaking news running the gamut from the bank robbery to politics and traffic problems. Where they differ, however, is with the features ("How to lose ten pounds without dieting," "How to revitalize your sex life with a phenomenal new natural herb"). It's all entertainment.

But, when it comes to entertainment segments or shows, it's "how well you dig." Who is going to get the latest "scoop" on Tom Hanks or Tom Cruise? Epstein had shown his ability as a digger, and the CBS station saw him as someone who could lift them out of the doldrums, as well as bring some entertainment flair to the news broadcast. The channel's news offerings were last in the ratings.

Epstein hit the top of the ladder when he was brought in as a show producer, with responsibility for building and laying out the news broadcast. "A lot of what airs you decide. Will it be a live shot, or just copy. Will you use the in-house anchor or a reporter? You assign the writers, create the graphic look."

News show, however, are not all the same. For someone eyeing the niche as a career, Epstein has some advice. Typically, most stations have a morning, afternoon, 5 and 11 P.M. entry. Each differs. "Noon news is like mini-evening version and contains some local plus national; 5 P.M. caters more to the female audience, because there are more of them home at that hour. There's usually a lot of medical news, physical fitness advice, and entertainment. At 6 P.M. we get bigger in terms of local news and at 11 P.M. the show gets sexier."

KEY ORGANIZATION CAN HELP

Epstein, a dual Emmy Award winner who has covered everything from the O.J. Simpson trial to bank shootouts, says a key organization for anyone to be aware of if they are trying to get into the business is the Radio, Television, News Directors Association (RTNDA), which holds seminars and an annual convention which is a great "job exchange." It's a place where most attendees bring tapes of their work and pursue opportunities.

"There are," says Epstein, "opportunities ranging from field producers in major markets to jack-of-all-trades in smaller markets." Epstein advises looking closely at the smaller markets. They are the places where "you can learn more than one thing. They are great places to also learn how people speak, the accents they have, and what the real difference is between the written and spoken word."

For anyone working in the entertainment environment, a major prerequisite is being able to differentiate between those written and spoken words. Epstein, who also won six Golden Mike awards, along with the Emmy for best daytime news producer and one for handling breaking news, says "be aware of what's going on around you. You never know when the break will come. When you see them, take advantage of it. They may not happen again."

For illustrator, animator, art director Bob Schulenberg, the breaks came more than once. While Epstein, Rose, and others steered a straight course toward their goals, Schulenberg floated through several different industries before he finally landed in entertainment. The turning point was when he gave up a promising, lucrative advertising career and returned to Los Angeles because of family health problems.

Los Angeles was not what Schulenberg had planned but "sometimes this business throws you a curve." When that happens, "just do your best to shake it off. Things don't always go the way we want, even in entertainment." Schulenberg, who had returned to the West Coast because his mother was ill, suddenly found things happening—big things.

BEHIND THE PRODUCTION DESIGNER

Through some of his friends (once again, the importance of networking), his skill with art work covering the 1920s came to the attention of Zoetrope Studios (owned by Francis Ford Coppola). As it turned out, the coordinator of Coppola's art department was an old schoolmate of Schulenberg. That's all it took. Within a short time, he became the production designer for *Hammett*, a film made by Coppola in the early 1980s.

The key to the production designer's job is design and artistic ability. Often, there is no clearly defined lines as to what they will or will not do. Usually, as in Schulenberg's case, the production designer organizes the art department and works with the director to determine what is needed. "When you get to this stage, there is a lot of overlap and confusion with production designers, how they work with art directors, illustrators, directors, and others. I had photo and costume design background which helped as well. The broader the background you have, the more experience you have gone through, the greater the opportunity and the value you will have to the production."

With his skills, Schulenberg soon found himself in demand. Instead of one motion picture, he was doing four. The diverse education and learning experience paid off. He had finally hit it, big, but other things were still to come. In the midst of his success, Schulenberg, producer Paul Bartel, and a group of other friends got together and decided to do their own motion picture. It was the early 1980s and although film budgets were nothing like they are today, they were still significant. Unfortunately, Schulenberg and friends were unable to raise the money, so they did the next best thing. They worked during the week and shot the film on weekends. They raised the money they needed, often just a few hours before it was spent.

LOW BUDGET CLASSIC

The low budget film, however, turned out to be a classic. Called *Eating Raoul*, it turned out to be a landmark film for both Schulenberg and those involved in it. It was the hit of the Los Angeles Film Festival, and later won the New York Film Festival.

Eating Raoul, Schulenberg says, taught him a great deal about New York and Los Angeles, and what it takes to make it in each area. In Manhattan, huge crowds saw *Eating Raoul* and in Los Angeles few people even heard about it. Much of it has to do with geography. In New York, everyone knows each other. Los Angeles is big and spread out. So are the friendships. "If you're a singer," he says, "go to New York where everyone knows what's happening in the clubs."

Schulenberg says there are certain rules that those trying to enter the business should keep in mind. They worked for him and made a significant difference in his career. First, "analyze what you want to do and hang around with those who do it. If you are dealing with publications, go where they are. If you want to get into stage work, go to New York; for motion pictures, go to Los Angeles. Go where the action is."

Action is what every potential entertainment industry hopeful waits for. Sometimes it happens, sometimes it doesn't, and sometimes it happens years later. That's the way it was for Chuck Bowman, an extremely talented producer/director. Initially, he wanted to be an actor but one day the reality hit. He was in his thirties and not getting any starring roles, although he had done more than two dozen television shows.

But, Bowman chose wisely. He gave up acting and went to work for Stephen J. Cannell, one of the most prolific creators of television series. From that point, his career moved rapidly. He worked in a trio of key positions—producing, executive producer, and director. Initially, he was an associate producer for *Baa Baa Blacksheep*, then he moved to creator Ken Johnson (*Incredible Hulk* and V), where he continued to pile on the producing credits. Then, Johnson gave Bowman the opportunity to direct.

The thing about producing, executive producing, and directing—like many other titles in entertainment—is there are no clear division of duties. Unlike a chief financial officer of a company who handles all the money, a director, producer, and executive producer has overlapping duties. What a director does for one company, he might not do for another.

THE DIFFERENCE IN EPISODIC TV

Bowman worked primarily in episodic television—that is, episodes from series. "Normally, the executive producer in episodic television is the person who has created the series for the network and is generally a writing producer. Directing is storytelling. More than just technical awareness, the director has to have his or her head into storytelling. That's the toughest and most important part of the job."

The director also has to be attuned to the mechanical aspect of shooting but "you learn that primarily by doing," he says. Regardless of what position someone has (producer, director, or executive producer) "you have to be more critical in television because you have less time and less help. Feature films generally have more time and assistance. There's much more opportunity to fix things.

"Frankly, to begin, I was not a good director, but I'm learning." Apparently, he has learned quickly. He's been directing episodes of The Pretender, VIP, and also has a motion picture scheduled for ABC.

"Entertainment is not like going to medical school, where everyone has a similar education. People in this business come from every walk of life and they do not follow any particular pattern. That's one of the things that makes it so interesting. If you listen to the many different people in this business, you learn a great deal."

Casey Kasem was one of those who listened intently to others. "I discovered things like there are 25 different ways to deliver a line. Often it is just a difference in attitude. Take, for instance, Union Oil's 'Spirit of '76' spot." How do you get 25 approaches? "Try," Kasem explains, "saying it like a father-to-son; bank president to employee; angry, sexy, tongue-in-cheek, and so on. Practice every different approach you can imagine.

"Softening a key word makes it stand out, as does laying back with it or raising your voice level. By the way, don't clear your throat before speaking because you will sound less like an announcer. Leaving the garbage (saliva) in makes a young voice sound older, and has a guy-next-door or man-on-the-street effect. Adopt the attitude that fits.

"Attitude," he says, "shapes your believability, and it is the most important thing you can bring to a commercial. The listener may not buy everything you tell him, but they can appreciate the fact you are talking to them like an adult." They also appreciate the fact the announcer "believes" in what they are selling.

"Treat a commercial as something you are introducing to someone that might help him, the way a grocer points out a new product to a customer. When you find yourself selling something you really like, give it your best. Treat every spot you deliver as something significant. Remember, to take time to do something with the copy that no one else has done."

One way to get a foot in the door is practicing with public service commercials. Every radio station in the country airs PSAs and, for the most part, they are canned (prerecorded). But, why not ask the station manager about delivering them yourself? That's much more likely to happen in a smaller market, where competition is not as intense and station managers are not worried as much about what the outlet down the street is doing.

IMPORTANCE OF TAPING SPOTS

But, just stopping at the station and asking doesn't guarantee you are going to get the spot. Kasem recommends practice, practice, and more practice. Tape your spots, listen and compare them to those you hear on the air. The tape is a must for anyone wanting to go beyond local radio. Landing commercials and announcing jobs in major markets will take an agent, but in order to get one, a demo tape is a must.

Kasem recommends putting two or three versions of a spot on the tape. Read them differently. Give the agent an idea of your ability and flexibility. "You won't build a career," says Kasem, "in voice-over unless you have an agent. Another key element in establishing a career is meeting people who can help you. That is not going to happen in a rural area. You need to be where things are happening. Above all, look for something special in every spot you read. Don't just read spots, look for something—a word, phrase—that will help you make that spot sound better than it ever has."

Personal manager Paul Addis' ideas about commercials have set him apart and taken his management company to a new level. One that could shake up the profession. Addis has shown what someone, with relatively few resources, can do to carve a niche in the business. Instead of getting an agent to represent his artists and find work for the performers, Addis is involved himself.

For instance, Addis has started to put together a series of home videos that are corporate sponsored. The films are usually tied to the sponsor. An example is one that he shot about the Jewish holidays. It is a "Jewish holiday video guide," he explains. "In other words, it takes you through the different holidays, talks about each, and gives the viewer insight into them. It's not a news show, but more along the lines of entertainment. Hebrew National sponsored it and paid for the entire project. Consumers of Hebrew National products then found discount coupons for the videos in their purchases. They could send in the discount coupon and get a video. When they view the video, they find it not only has a tour of the holidays, but a few kind words about Hebrew National."

The advantage: Hebrew National has a premium item to offer customers, it comes off as almost public service and not commercial, because it is not selling anything. So, Hebrew National supplies a product, makes a small profit, and enhances its image among customers. A second film is sponsored by a drug company and is safety-oriented and geared toward children. The product is cough medicine. As is the case with the Hebrew National film, Addis not only shoots the film, but uses his clients in it whenever possible.

Of course, shooting film of Jewish holidays, or being behind the camera for a safety film, and working a promotional tie with Hebrew National is not your typical managerial duty. But, Addis says the business is changing. He was brought up as a salesman, and landed his first job in retail sales when he was 15 years of age.

A Need for Change

"Managers are going to have to carefully examine those changes and see if they shouldn't be doing things differently. I think they have to . . . no business, even one as traditional as entertainment, stays the same." Jay Lowy saw need for change in music publishing. After more than a decade in it, he saw an opportunity that few realized. "Motown Records and Jobette Music (the company that published most of the Motown hits) had turned out one multimillion-selling record after another, and the publishing company enjoyed some good royalties. The recordings not only were hits in the Black market, but they also sold extremely well to the White consumer. My thought was to take the Jobette catalog—which primarily consisted of songs from Motown's stable of Black artists—and get the songs recorded by non-Black singers."

That's exactly what Lowy did. His career took off along with the revenue from the Jobette catalog and for the next decade he headed the publishing company and made it one of the best-known and most profitable in the world.

Under Lowy's direction, Jobette also introduced "one-stop shopping" for licensing. That is, anyone who wants to use a tune has to license it from the publisher. Lowy's idea was that you could license both recording, film, and soundtrack rights with one license. No one else was doing it and, once again, Jobette's revenues took off.

Lowy says there is enormous opportunity in publishing. "For instance, there are more sources of income from publishing today than ever before. We have cable, satellite, home video. Those are only a few. Who knows what is coming—the Internet. If you get into this business, you should be looking for those things. Don't just be a representative for a song publisher. Do a little creative thinking and you'll be amazed where this business can take you. Every publisher is looking for someone with imagination and drive."

ADVERTISEMENT CHANGES CAREER

Drive is what Tisha Fein has enormous amounts of. Her career turned when she answered an ad and became a receptionist for a public relations firm (in Los Angeles) that handled many of the book promotion tours that authors took.

As things developed, those within the firm began to realize that when an author came to town, the one person in the office who had the most rapport with them was the outgoing Tisha. They began to assign her authors and publicity tours. "I was driving a beat-up VW and carting around a host of celebrity authors."

It appeared as if Tisha was going to make a career out of PR, but things changed. "I got married, moved to Philadelphia, and went to work for the Marsha Rose show, one of the first local television issue-oriented talk shows." Tisha was a natural. With her artist rapport, she brought on a host of guests including Woodward/Bernstein.

"A good talent coordinator is someone who can track talent. You might have an idea who you want, but how do you reach them. In many cases, you also have to convince them to come on the show," she explains. Tisha was exceptionally good at getting the hard-to-get talent out of hiding. She left the Rose show and began to freelance as a coordinator and among those she is particularly proud of in finding (and booking)—Brian Wilson of the Beach Boys who "came out of his sandbox to appear" on a syndicated show (*Sessions*) she was booking.

But that's not where it ended. Tish's reputation began to build, especially after she landed stars like Harry Nielsen and Stevie Wonder. She worked for Dick Clark and helped put together his network specials for the next year then she landed the Grammys—and for the past 20 years she has been the coordinating producer/talent coordinator.

THE PEOPLE CONNECTION

What does she credit her rise to? "If you are going to get into this business, you have to be good with people. At ease with them. It helps to have a sense of humor, don't take no for an answer—because many celebrity guests initially tell you that—and keep your ears to the ground."

That means, pay attention to what's happening in the business. One of the outstanding things about Tisha is she usually knows which guests are the hot ones before anyone else. "I read and listen to what's going on in the industry."

Tony Selznick has done the same thing. He has carefully watched the trends in dance and choreography, and he saw the need to specialize as an agent. Selznick, who got his dancing/choreography background from music videos ("I was casting them"), was asked to do the casting for *Cop Rock* based on the success of the music videos.

Cop Rock, a dramatic musical based on the success of music videos, was the turning point in Selznick's career. "We had tons of dancers in every episode, and that's where I saw the value of casting and the dancing background." Thus, Selznick went into the casting business, concentrating on dancing and choreography.

"Everything is a specialty today. Niche marketing is in. If I had just gone into casting, I would be another agent out there fighting for the same thing. But, by offering only dancers and choreographers, we have become the place where people come when they need someone along those lines. Being a specialist in the business has become a key to success." It has also made Selznick's agent the first place that production companies go when they need dancers and/or choreographers.

MORE OPPORTUNITY TODAY

Selznick believes there is more opportunity in the business for others who are eyeing the same approach. In fact, dance has become so popular that some agencies—like Selznick's—are even specializing within the agency. "For instance, one of our biggest divisions supplies dancers in the over 50 category, and you would be amazed at the demand."

Selznick and others see that demand for dancers even growing more, as agencies get into the production business and dance/choreography impacts more people. "Credit MTV," he says, "for much of this craze. They have brought back dance and made it popular all over again."

They have also created a new opportunity and niche for anyone anxious to break into the agency and dance/choreography business. Thanks to behind-the-scenes performers such as Selznick, Huggins, Miller and others one other thing is obvious—there is room at the top.

CHAPTER FIVE

More Opportunities, Plus the Pitfalls, Money, and Future

W e turned down Steven Spielberg not once, but twice," says Dean Jewell, shaking his head slowly from side to side, "and if that doesn't say that entertainment is an inexact science then maybe this story will. Once we had a graduate student in class, a brilliant 4.0 scholar who had graduated from Harvard. He thought filmmaking was something he wanted to do, but he could not make a film to save his soul. He was probably too brainy for this medium."

Just a few miles west of the film school where Dean Jewell presides, is the well-known agency, William Morris. The agency has become noted for the well-known entertainment industry personalities who have worked their way from the Morris mailroom to the upper echelon of many well-known motion picture, television, and radio firms.

Stories about William Morris agents, managers, labels, producers, and directors who guessed wrong or who made mistakes are legendary. Ninety-five percent of all new products introduced in America fail, so it is no wonder that entertainment companies frequently sign the wrong person and drop the right one. Entertainment conglomerates are no different than other corporations. They can (and do) make mistakes and they frequently rush to judgment.

WHY WRITER WAS DROPPED

Screenwriter, telewriter Peter Lefcourt remembers his experience with being dropped well. Initially, he was the toast of the studio. Universal television executives flew him to California, supplied him with a decent advance (for the time), and then forgot he existed. When there was a shift in policy, the series was dropped, along with it Lefcourt.

None of that phased Lefcourt, until the agents—who had been calling him night and day—suddenly refused to take any of his calls. "Nobody remembers you the next day if something happens," says Lefcourt. In Lefcourt's case, most of those agents wish they had. He went on to win an Emmy for *Cagney & Lacey*.

Dean Jewell says "sell your first script or get that first assignment. Once you do, everything is much easier. That first break is the key." And, everyone wants you after that.

But, which comes first, the chicken or the egg? Does the person trying to get into the business have to hit it big before they get an agent? Or, are there agents out there who are willing to crapshoot and sign someone before they hit it big?

The truth is there are few crapshooters in the business because there are too many players. If you are a writer like Lefcourt, there are several options that translate to opportunities. He recommends writing a script on speculation (spec). "They are called audition scripts, when you talk about television," Lefcourt explains, "and they are often worth the effort."

Lefcourt says write one for an existing series. Don't do it with the expectations of selling. "Just hope someone who sees it will say you can really write." Writing for a series and on spec forces the hopeful author to see the elements in the television series and, hopefully, what the producers want. Once the script is written, Lefcourt says it is time to "pursue an agent. Get one. You rarely can sell a script without an agent."

WHERE PERSEVERANCE ENTERS

Agents read scripts, but you have to beat down their door. "This is where perseverance comes in. You can't be faint of heart," he says. "Get an agent to read it." They will—eventually. "There are so many scripts out there, and many agents who will consider an unproduced writer. But, you have to get to them and convince them."

About every third college student has a script in his pocket, and the ranks of the would-be writers in the Writer's Guild has gone from about 1,500 twenty-five years ago to more than 8,500 today. That does not mean the opportunity has thinned. On the contrary, it is evidence that there are more opportunities. Twenty-five years ago, the cable outlets were not the force they are today. So-called "fourth" networks were unheard of and the opportunity to sell scripts and ideas outside the big three (NBC, CBS, ABC) was virtually nonexistent. If you wrote a script on spec, most of your co-horts would say you needed your head examined.

But the entire outlook has changed. Today, there is a plethora of openings and needs. Last season, the networks' share of the total viewing audience dropped below 50 percent. "The business is changing," says Jewell, "and the opportunities in it." Jewell points out that when he started some 22 years ago, the industry thought of motion pictures as products that were made, marketed to theaters around the world, and once the release cycle was over, you had the opportunity to sell it to television networks and various foreign stations. But, that was the end of the line.

The entire picture has changed with cable and video. Many filmmakers make back their investment before the film is even in general release through foreign, cable, and video sales. There's also merchandising and promotional tradeouts (i.e., studios like Disney working deals with fast-food chains). So, there is more opportunity.

Jewell points out that nearly 80 years ago, David Sarnoff of RCA, envisioned an "umbrella" motion picture company. One that would embrace radio and theater (vaudeville) all under one roof. "Allow them to support each other symbiotically, and you would have something extraordinary insofar as a money-making enterprise." That's exactly what we have today, says Jewell. Companies like Sony own theaters, videotapes, and so on. A good chunk of the entertainment business—especially film—is going that way. Big companies are getting bigger, medium- and small-sized ones are being bought up.

WHY TIMING IS RIGHT

"Technology and cable television is exploding," says Jewell. "It's a good time to be thinking about getting into the industry. It is never going to be easy. It is one of the most competitive industries in the world, but there is going to be more and more need for product. And the nice thing is you do not have to be in Hollywood. New York has become a film center and there is work going on in many other places—Texas, Florida, Chicago, and so on. Los Angeles, though, remains dominant."

Jewell sees the day when someone can sit down at a computer and make a motion picture. "It may not be in 10 or 20 years, it may even take 50, but the day will come when a person will be able to sit down and make a feature film on the computer."

The hot area now is animation, says Jewell. "There seems to be more things being done that combine animation and real people. You can get into the area but remember it is tough. The people who ultimately make it are those who are willing to commit a portion of their lives knocking on doors. Many of them will even beg and ask to 'just be a production assistant on your film.' It takes PPCC—perseverance, personality, connections, and commitment."

Paul Addis agrees with Jewell's assessment, but thinks you need to add one more element to the mix. "Good business sense." Addis, a personal manager and principal of Ambitious Entertainment, has been in sales since he was 15 years of age, and believes salesmanship is a critical attribute for anyone who is trying to make it in the business. "We are all basically salespeople, and you need to have savvy in that area. You need to know how to get along with people, and you need to be versatile, see the new technology that is coming on stream and stay ahead of the game. The opportunity for inroads are tremendous."

None of that, however, guarantees you a job. What helps, says associate producer Jerad Grimes (MTV), who has his sights set on a producing position ("one of these days") is "ambition and drive. Next is connections with people in the industry who have the ability and connections to give you a job."

Most Important Step

Michelle Baxter, who as of this writing was one step ahead of Grimes (she went from associate producer to segment producer), believes the most important step in breaking into the business is "doing an internship. A lot of people in (or out) of college do not realize the value. They look at the immediate dollars, but that's wrong. They feel because they graduated they should be getting a high paying position. That does not happen. Six months of interning is often equivalent to a college education. The internship I served far exceeded anything I learned in school."

Ms. Baxter says there are internship opportunities available everywhere—and for everyone. Even age is not a barrier, although if you are 18 to 34, the odds of you getting an internship or breaking into the business are greater. Advertisers are hung up on reaching that age bracket, and feel if you are in that age group you may have a better insight into how to appeal to the 18 to 34. Michelle, as others do, points to the growing number of cable outlets and the massive amounts of airtime many of the stations need to fill.

"Go where you find interest. If it is MTV, go there. Be aware, too, that everything is getting more specialized. You'll find news and cooking channels, and who would have thought that an all-weather channel would ever make it. Many of these stations hire interns, and it usually lasts for three or four months. But, if you land one of those positions and you work hard, by the time the internship is up, you will probably be able to land something more permanent. Approach the human resource department of the show (if there is one) or the station."

Michelle says there is more opportunity on the West Coast than New York. Even better than either coast are local stations. "Face it, the station in Des Moines, Iowa, may be more accessible than the one in New York or Los Angeles. Local stations are the place to start, and preferably those that are in smaller markets."

How to Use Local Outlet

Multimedia website producer Erick Finke knows the value of the local outlet. The local television cable channel in his (New England) area had promised (as many cable stations do) to produce a certain amount of local community shows. But they had no staff to produce, direct, write, or develop the shows. Erick volunteered. It wasn't easy.

Three days a week the station started airing at 5:30 in the morning, and from 6:45 to 7:15 A.M. there was an aerobics show that was hosted by an ambitious secretary in the market. Erick and his partner started off as floor managers (the people who are on-stage that talk to the director with earphones). The station had two cameras, and Erick learned everything, from handling the camera to taking orders from the director as to where people should move, stand, and so on. Then he became assistant director (the person who sits with the director and executes his orders).

Erick did this job for a year and even developed a public affairs news show. "We started developing our own topics, too. Nuclear energy was the lowest rated, while two local high school coaches talking about the upcoming big game was the highest.

WHAT SELLS AND WHAT DOESN'T

"It gave us a taste of reality, what sells and what does not. It also taught us a valuable lesson—what you like isn't necessarily what the audience wants, and what you think isn't necessarily what the audience is thinking. For instance, we always thought the people watching the aerobics show were housewives and others interested in a morning workout. From the call-ins, we discovered that the prime audience was senior citizen males who liked watching this shapely 19-year-old with her tights going through the exercise routine."

Those senior citizens threw the projected demographics from advertising agencies into a dither. Normally, agencies segment shows into fine-tuned niches and hope to tell advertisers exactly how many prime, 18- to 34-year-olds they have viewing. The penchant for segmentation has created enormous new opportunity for casting directors, the people who specialize in finding the talent to fill the demographic needs of the agency or production company.

Production companies/agencies come to casting directors in search of specific talent to appeal to an exact demographic group.

Casting agents have a lucrative practice as well, but they differ from the typical agent. The agent usually has an artist(s) signed to them and they have to not only find work for their people, but act as managers, as well. Thus, many have opted for the casting director role in which the agent works for an agency, studio, or production company and has no obligation to specific talents.

As advertisers get more niche-oriented and scientific, the openings for these "scouts" grows. Nancy McCook of Anderson Casting views the future as filled with opportunity for the prospective casting director. The place to start—casting offices as interns, or the Academy of Arts and Sciences also has an internship program.

TRAINING PROGRAMS AVAILABLE

"Agencies," says Ms. McCook, "often have a training program. William Morris does. Or, get in on the ground floor of a production company. Either way, this job offers an excellent shot at developing a good career."

Breaking into entertainment, however, is not like getting a shot at the retail clerks, the computer department of a major company, or anything else. Often, in business, when you perform above and beyond the norm you catch the eye of the boss and earn brownie points. They mark you as an up-and-comer. Not too many prospective executives earn this tag.

In entertainment, going above and beyond the norm is not a rarity or something that earns you points. It is, at the very least, expected. Those who do not go the extra mile are written off. Grimes says "always be prepared to go above and beyond. In this business, you are frequently at the whim of a network, producer, or someone who is under a great deal of pressure. If they see you are someone who does not put out 200 percent, they are quick to forget you."

Grimes points out that the people you are competing against are not the normal, run-of-the-mill, average workers or executives. "They are committed. Remember, many have given up well-paying professions to work for minimum wage. They are not going to give in easily, and most will work their tail off to make an impression on a producer, director, or someone else with the power to keep them around."

To make those contacts and to open the doors, Ms. Baxter says it is important to make sure that "people know what you do. It does no good to work hard if no one knows you are, and if they haven't the foggiest notion of what you do. Some people would call it beating your chest or pounding the drums. You have to, but use subtleness."

THERE'S MORE TO THE BUSINESS THAN WORK

There is more to the business than just working hard and getting ahead. You have to be objective in evaluating your skills and abilities. It does no good to work your way up to a key production assignment and suddenly discover you cannot do it. Erick Finke got himself in that position when he worked for a nonprofit organization that put together anti-nuclear films. Finke worked on one and discovered "I certainly was not a director, nor did I have the skills to become one. I could see I was a good producer. I could organize things and get them in order and ready."

That was a turning point for Finke. He had always envisioned himself as capable of doing everything behind-the-scenes, but after working on a production, he discovered that was not true. "Make the most of your opportunities, but don't take one you are not equipped to fill."

Jeff Olds got involved in a documentary that was being done in Russia. He landed the position as associate producer, which meant he had to log all the material that was used, and make sure it was all running smoothly. That job required someone who was detail-oriented—Jeff wasn't. "It was the nightmare of my life," he recalls, "and the producer hated my work. I couldn't blame him. After all, I was goofing up his production. So, if an opportunity arises, take it—as long as it does not require you to go in over your head."

Interestingly, entertainment, which is frequently thought of as one of the most creative industries in the country, resembles a copycat business. For instance, if three or four comedy series suddenly hit it big on television, everyone starts to make them. If science fiction motion pictures begin to score well at the box office, a plethora of science fiction films will hit the market.

TRENDS AND OPPORTUNITIES

Pick out an entertainment trend and you will find an opportunity. Tony Selznick, who found a niche in the business by becoming a choreographers' agent, points to several. "Last year, *The Drew Carey Show* booked a choreographer, and the ratings were so high that *3rd Rock from the Sun* called, booked another dance episode—and it won an Emmy."

Selznick, who took advantage of the trend in which agents specialize, says there are opportunities in handling choreographers and dancers but the way these artists are being handled "is nothing like they were in the 1940s and 1950s. Back then, you might be watching a film and suddenly the stars would break into song and dance for no reason. Today, that doesn't go. What's acceptable to audiences is a situation where the dance or choreography fits, it's natural. For instance, in *Scent of a Woman* the tango number fit naturally. It wasn't forced, it was part of the action. That's where the future of the business—and booking choreographers and dancers—appears to be."

But, how does an agent find out who is doing a production that needs choreographers/dancers. "If you are running a dance/choreography agency, you need to be proactive. In the old days, studios would come searching for the talent, that is no longer true. We search out every job opportunity."

By that, Selznick means the agent has to look through the daily "breakdowns" that agents receive every morning. They describe who is casting what, but rarely do they say "choreography. Instead it might say something about a romantic comedy about a guy and his girlfriend and her ex-fiance." A breakdown with that—or similar—wording is a clue to Selznick that this is probably a romantic comedy and they may need choreographers and dancers. Selznick says in many cases the production company may put out the breakdown and not even be aware they need a choreographer. It is only when the agency approaches them that "a light goes on and they realize this is going to take dancers and choreography."

In many cases, it is the dance numbers that turn out to be the memorable part of the feature. "*Austin Powers*," says Selznick, "is one." Aside from not recognizing when they need a choreographer, production companies try to avoid having their films branded as dance or choreographed productions because of the stigma. Unlike the Fred Astaire/Ginger Rogers days, today's musicals (when they are filmed and released) more often than not turn out to be stiffs. Until the industry has a few dance films that do well at the box office, production companies will shy away from branding any motion picture as a musical or dance production.

CRISIS IN DANCE MOVIES

Selznick says "one of his clients was doing several dance and musical numbers in Jim Carrey's *The Mask*, but to keep the studio from getting upset he told them he was making a horror film (much more acceptable) disguised as a musical." In 1999, *Dream Girls* was slated to be released as a musical, but when *Why Do Fools Fall in Love?* did poorly at the box office, *Dream Girls* was shelved.

One interesting note about choreography and dance is that production companies often do not even realize they have a need for it. Selznick explains that when he searches through the breakdowns, he rarely ever finds choreography as a line item. "Ninety percent of the time we get a call from the production manager the day before the filming is to take place. They suddenly realize they need choreography, but they haven't even provided a budget for it." Often the director literally "turns the set over to the choreographer and asks him how he wants to do it. There is tremendous opportunity for the person who understands how the business is changing, the trends and how they fit in."

Selznick—and other specialized agents—could well be a private investigators. So could talent coordinators such as Tish Fein. Fein credits her ability to track people (and have rapport with them once she finds them) as a key reason for her success. Ms. Fein, who has hunted up talent for shows as diverse as *Dick Clark*, *The Image Awards*, and the *Grammys*, says the way to break into the business is to volunteer.

"Try a telethon where you not only see how the show is put together, but you have the opportunity to meet the production people as well as those who are in front of the camera. There's nothing like a telethon to make connections."

Every telethon can use people that will answer the telephone, run errands, handle messages for some of the personalities, even be a valet. Telethons need volunteers. "In fact," recalls Ms. Fein, "I have a friend who volunteered on several telethons and he became the talent coordinator for the *Hollywood Christmas Parade*. The receptionist who worked for me at *Solid Gold* is now a vice president at MTV."

Developing Contacts

More than anything, breaking into the business as a talent coordinator involves developing contacts, and one other thing—not being in awe of those you meet who are in the business. Ms. Fein grew up in the industry (her father was Irving Fein, a well-known manager who handled a number of prominent artists like Jack Benny and George Burns), and feels at home around celebrities. To feel at home around the personalities she deals with almost daily (everyone from Aretha Franklin to Elton John and the Bee Gees), Ms. Fine says you have to keep your private and work life separate. She has two personalities.

"If I go to a party," she explains, "you might find me to be shy and withdrawing. Parties are not my thing, I don't have to perform there. But, if I have a show to put together and talent to gather, my personality changes. I am no longer shy." To get into the business and stay in it, you may have difficulty with a one-dimensional personality. If you are soft-spoken, easy-going, and prone to being alone, this business may not be for you. Ms. Fein (and others) are used to being with people (i.e., the talent they book, the show hosts they deal with). That takes an outgoing personality. However, no one expects you to be outgoing and re-lationship-oriented 24 hours a day. That might burn you out, even in entertainment. "There has to be a time when you can relax and be yourself."

If there is any phase of the entertainment industry that has potential, and is seldom thought about it is song publishing. Both the opportunity and income derived rival anything in the business. Jay Lowy, a longime veteran of the business and for-mer president of the National Academy of Recording Arts and Science (NARAS), knows it well. Lowy has spent his entire career in song publishing, and he has never seen anything in the in-dustry to rival it for opportunity and earning potential. It is one of those businesses where you do not need to read or write music, yet those who are involved in it deal with every top singer (and songwriter) in the country.

"It is the most valuable income generator in all entertain-ment," says Lowy. "Think about this—while many things both in and out of the entertainment industry depreciate in value, copyrights rarely ever go down in value, and generating in-come requires the lowest investment of any phase of enter-tainment. To give you an idea of how significant the dollars are, when Kirk Kikorian wanted to build the MGM hotel in Las Vegas, he sold MGM's publishing to back the financing. It was MGM's prime asset."

But there is a caveat. "You need to live in one of the three major music centers," says Lowy. "However, if you live in New York, Los Angeles, or Nashville and want to get into entertainment, this is one business you should not ignore."

How Do You Break into Music Publishing?

So, how do you break into it? Simple, says Lowy. There is the record label route. Many companies hire interns as do major publishers. Even if a label or publisher does not hire one, there is every opportunity to land an internship by talking to the manager of the publishing house and the label's human resource department. In today's environment, both are overworked and looking for help. Interns do not make significant salaries, and often they work for nothing. That's an offer that a label and publishing house would have a hard time refusing.

"I know the term is overused," says Lowy, "but the key is you need to 'hang out' and meet people. You might even get a job as a promoter (radio) and move into song publishing that way. Promotion people learn publishing, and they see the potential."

Music publishing companies often go for the younger "song plugger," a term used to describe the publishing representative, hence the name. Lowy came up that way, only he started at the bottom rung—he was a sales clerk in a music store while he went to school. As soon as he graduated high school, he was offered a job as a radio promotion man. The offer came from the manager of the music store, who had moved on to radio but was familiar with Lowy's enthusiasm and work ethic.

Lowy says it is still possible for youngsters breaking into the market to get into radio, but the promotion business has changed significantly.

"In those days, promotion was prehistoric," Lowy laughs. "All they did was give me a box of records and a telephone directory."

The directory was for Lowy to look up radio stations, get their address, and make a promotion call.

THE VISION THAT IS NEEDED

"You never knew what kind of station you were going to visit, because the telephone directory did not define it. Once, I ended up visiting a religious broadcaster with a box full of pop records. The prime benefit of the job was that it led me to other more lucrative parts of the business, such as publishing. You have to be able to see the opportunities and be willing to take a job that may not be that great in hopes of learning the business."

What Lowy and others make clear is that all these entry opportunities had two characteristics. They were, almost without exception, low-paying and often short-lived. That's why Andy Epstein says "do it while you are young. You cannot be worried about security. When you go to work for a network, you hope it is healthy, and if it is you will continue to have a job. But, whether it is or not, the important thing is you never can worry about tenure, pensions, or longevity. That's not the nature of the business."

Although nearly every aspect of the business is wide open for interns, commercial announcers such as Casey Kasem and Robert Brown say that interning is not the way to break into the voice-over field. "Submit a tape," they both advise, "to an agent." It is only through an agent that voice-over people get work, and for a good reason. Voice-over agents deal with advertising agencies, and it is the agency that actually gives the commercial announcer a job (or commercial spot to cut).

Agencies do not want to be flooded by voice-over people who are trying to break into the business. They want to talk to qualified announcers, and the feeling is that an agent will screen the prospective voice-over people before he submits the tape and the person to an agency.

They are right. Agents make a living by not only providing advertising agencies with qualified, talented people, but they know if they should start submitting people who were not qualified, the client (agency) would soon lose faith in them. Income is predicated on the confidence an ad agency has in the agent. If the agent "burns" the agency too much, that confidence will disappear, and with it the agent and his commercial client.

DON'T FORGET THE TAPE

Kasem recommends sending the agent as simple a tape as possible of what you can do. It does not have to be an aired commercial. Nor does it need to be something with music in the background and 40 different dialects. One 30-second spot can suffice, but it should be what you do best. Take a commercial from the radio and read it. Regardless of where you get it, make it something you can do comfortably without forcing it. Try to make the spot something you feel at home with. If your voice has a nostalgic quality to it, do a spot with nostalgia in it. The prime thing the agent wants to hear is if you can convince him to buy that product.

Regardless of whether someone has a demo tape or not, commercials—and breaking into them—is not easy. Some people think that all it takes is to step up to the microphone and read—nothing could be more misleading.

Before submitting your tape to an agent, Brown recommends a few things. "If you want to get into the business, the first thing you should do is get a recording machine (cassette) with a good microphone. That's important. Listen to what you are doing. Read short stories with short sentences. They are frequently like commercials, and they will help you get the timing right. You can rent studio time in off-hours for a reasonable fee."

Casey says, "you have to be in the middle of what is going on. The most common mistake, and the thing that holds you up the most in the business, is that people read the spot instead of looking for something in it to make it better. Take time to do something with the copy no one else has done. That can impress an agent."

When Brown first entered the field, there were few actors involved. Since then, actors have realized the size of the income voice-over people make and they have jumped into the field. But, Casey cautions that merely sounding like an actor and having a deep voice is no guarantee you will get commercial work.

Casey makes an interesting point about deep resonant voices. "A big deep voice makes you sound like every other announcer. You find yourself concentrating less on characterization and more on your deep voice, especially if you have an acting background. If you have an acting background and feel you can read broadcast spots, consider yourself in the running. Take what you have, make it work for you—then apply your acting skills to voice-overs."

If audiocassettes are a prerequisite for commercial announcers, does it help to send a canned video of your work to television stations in hopes of catching someone's attention? Les Rose says "definitely. That's how most photojournalists get their jobs."

Rose, who sent five resumes and five tapes to major Los Angeles television stations, says that still might not be enough. Much depends on the market you are after. If you are hoping to latch onto a station in a major market, you need a track record (as evidenced by your video), and usually you have to be located in the market area.

When Rose tried to get a job in Los Angeles, he was 3,000 miles away—which shows the opportunity is there and it can be done—if you have a video. Rose landed the job on his third try and impressed the manager with the quality of the tape, and his bold offer to visit, at his expense, the station for an interview.

But, where does someone get a tape if they are just starting out in the business? Stations in smaller markets, according to Rose, are ideal. They are open to bringing in young, aggressive photojournalists as interns. There is great opportunity at the cable level, too. Cable stations are growing rapidly, and most are short-handed (and lack the funds) to bring in full-time news cameramen and/or photojournalists. Nearly all are willing to listen to someone who is anxious to provide intern services. If you are an intern at a station, as Rose was, the opportunity is there.

NEED FOR A MENTOR

"Obviously, someone at the station has to let you shoot footage. That's not going to happen unless you build relationships and pick a mentor at the station," says Rose. "That is someone you run your tail off for, who appreciates what you are trying to do. I made friends with the anchorman on my station, plus I was the best intern—hardest working—the station ever had. Consequently, I got to go out on some stories with the regular photojournalists."

Going out on assignment does not happen unless you push. And nobody pays attention to your aggressiveness unless they see you are a hard worker, willing to go the extra mile. That means working extra hours, "hanging around" after your shift is over, and asking people if there is anything you can do if you find yourself with spare time. Or, as Rose says, "just schmoozing."

"Those things may sound mundane and simple, but think about your reaction to people who go the extra mile where you are working. If there is a promotion, they usually get it." Rose also is a big fan of thank-you notes. When applying for a job, whether it is as an intern or not, send a note after the interview. "Make it a positive letter, thank them for their continued consideration, which says you are still in the running. There are many things you can do to make sure they remember you. What you do when you apply for a position is an indicator of how good you may be as a photojournalist.

"Good photojournalists do not take no for an answer, and the station manager is going to be thinking about that when he gets your thank-you note. At the same time, do not push to the point where you bug the manager. Whenever you contact them, it should not just be to see if you are still in the running or to see if they have made a decision. That gets old. Don't contact them unless you have something new or of value to offer, for example, a new piece of film you shot that you thought would be of interest."

Video Workshop Available

Another area of opportunity and strong networking possibilities is the National Press Photographers Association (NPPA) video workshop. Usually, all the network heavyweights—the president of CBS News—is there along with the best photojournalists in the country. Along with them are opportunistic students who descend on the gathering because of the networking potential. There is a fee (around $75) to join, but it is well worth it, says Rose.

Richard Alvarez says the networking you do—whether it is at your local cable station, a network affiliate, or the NPPA—has to be supported by your ability. "By that, I mean the film you shoot has to reveal that you have an 'eye' for the story. That takes time to learn, but after awhile it should be a sixth sense. If you have that ability, people will see it in your footage, and you will have a future in this business."

Alvarez points out there is more competition today, but there are also more outlets. New cable stations (and entertainment shows) pop up daily. Another chance to break into the field is by freelancing. Stations need good footage, and there have been many cutbacks at stations. They do not have the labor they once had, and they are also getting more competition from cable and satellite outfits. Film—the element that makes television successful—is in demand and many stations rely on freelancers to cover events for them. Whichever way a prospective photojournalist goes, they should always "be thinking about what they are shooting and asking themselves," says Alvarez, "will this make a good story? Can I envision it on the evening news?"

Both Rose and Alvarez also emphasize the importance of being familiar with the station or show for which you are shooting. Does the film (and story) match their format? Not all this happens overnight. "Photojournalists learn by doing. That's one of the keys, especially when you shoot entertainment news. You need to show your ability so whenever you have the opportunity, think differently. Visualize shots from another perspective. This is a creative position and, although many people have the basics, they need to hone and refine them. That only comes with practice, practice, and more practice."

Producer/director Chuck Bowman says regardless of where you start, "one of the exciting things about this business is "you can go where you want. Internships or entry level positions are opportunities for a variety of entertainment industry careers." Bowman, who started as a page at NBC is evidence of that.

EVALUATING YOUR SKILLS

Bowman says one of the first things he did before he looked for any openings was to "evaluate his skills. That way, you know where you should be heading. Wherever you are, objectively measure the tools you have and what level your craft is on. There are plenty of places to get started. Too often we overlook the obvious. For instance, if you want to be a television producer or director, that does not mean you have to start in television. Radio is an excellent springboard as well, and many radio stations are controlled by people who also have an ownership in a local television station. That's how I got started. With the explosion in television and the resurgence of radio, there are great positions open.

"Remember, you have to get into the ballpark before you can play the game. So start anywhere. One thing builds on another. Even when things look hopeless, there is hope. I can only point to Randy Wallace. He wanted to get into the business, but just could not get anything going. He finally decided he was going to write a script regardless of what anyone said. He did and the result was *Brave Heart*."

Animation is far removed from *Brave Heart*, but Craig Miller says the success of so many studios other than Disney, has made animators an occupation that is in demand. The amount of animated material on the air is growing. There are ads for animators almost daily in the newspaper, however, Miller, who came up through the marketing end of the business, says that in entertainment you should always remember that "people hire people they like. If they don't know you they can't ever form an opinion, so get around."

But you don't have to be an animator in order to break into the field. Miller says that even if you "just have an animation idea, if the company likes it, they may hire someone to develop it—and you are in the door." He suggests that anyone trying to get into the field remember two things—first it is a business. That means a studio or production company is not going to go for any script if they do not feel it is commercial and will attract viewers.

Secondly, tastes (and studio executives) change almost daily. If someone praises your idea one day, and they are gone the next, don't be too disappointed. It happens. It happened more than once to production designer Bob Schulenberg. But, despite the disappointments, Schulenberg has had a great time with a variety of experiences.

Schulenberg looks at the industry and the chances of breaking into it realistically. "There are no studios anymore, but that does not mean the opportunity went with them. If you want to get into production design, I recommend going to independent filmmakers. For the most part, I think people have an excellent chance of hooking on as a production assistant. They won't be paid much, but they will learn. Even if you have to work for nothing on a film, do it. It will probably be the hardest work you ever do, but well worth it."

Schulenberg is also a great believer in going where the action is. If you want to be a production designer or writer, stay in Hollywood. "If you want to be a filmmaker, you can do a lot of things on a low budget. It does not take millions to make a film."

Independents will help. Paramount will frequently lend independent filmmakers props at no cost. Panasonic frequently supplies cameras. Even some of the stars are willing to work for minimum if they can own a piece of the film.

While some may question anyone's ability to make a film without a multimillion dollar budget and financing, Schulenberg simply points out *Eating Raoul*, the black comedy he and others did in Hollywood with minimal capital. "At the time, we thought we were making an underground film, but in reality we were making an independent film.

"If you have a camera, film, and enough money, you can finish a film and enter it in film festivals. If the project gets rave reviews—as *Eating Raoul* did—then you will get distribution. So, even though things have gotten expensive, it is entirely possible for someone who has never before made a film, to make one and be a success."

PITFALLS AND THE FUTURE

Getting a foothold in the business is not without its problems. As is the case with most businesses, the entertainment industry has its share of pitfalls. Take, for instance, writer Peter Lefcourt. He voices the problem that most in the entertainment field face—"there is no security. I've been doing it for 25 years, and I like the freedom. It's a tradeoff, and I don't think I would ever change this environment for the corporate world."

Writers face other obstacles in Hollywood and New York. One of the most recent is the growing number of college students who are hitting the industry with scripts. When Lefcourt started in the business, there were 1,500 hopeful writers in the Guild. Today, there are nearly 9,000. However, in addition, there is a growing number of independent television stations, both cable and others, who are buying scripts for local (and satellite) consumption.

While the numbers are growing, Lefcourt says he still has a hard time making any "long-term purchases. But, the lifestyle is well worth it."

Michelle Baxter, who has been both an associate and segment producer, says there are "no, no's." That is, in contrast to what many people believe, those in the profession frequently have to be as careful of what they say as their corporate counterparts. Ms. Baxter points out that there are some within the industry who will do anything to advance—"sometimes over a friend's body. In an industry as competitive as this one—with the potential rewards—that is not surprising." Still, Ms. Baxter "would not trade it for anything. This business is a lot of fun, and I can't imagine anything that even comes close."

Personal manager Paul Addis looks at the business more pragmatically and from a manager's perspective. "There are both pluses and minuses in working for yourself. Although the potential is in the six- and seven-figure range, you often do not have any consistency in income."

It is also a business that can be seasonal. Additionally, dealing with artists and musicians, you run into "people who have quirks. A personal manager gets more involved." Personal managers have pressure from another area—they have to keep artists employed. It's like the Los Angeles Lakers. If they do not do well, the coach will go. The same is true in personal management. If you have a client who feels they are not working enough, or not getting the right roles, the manager may be the person to go."

PLUS OR MINUS—FOREIGN FILM COMPANIES

Walking in Addis' shoes is not easy, because aside from all the personalities he handles, he also works with nearly 80 Asian film companies that supply work for his clients. That can be another plus and minus. It is a sales tool to utilize when you are going after clients, but if there is a slowdown in the Far East economy—

as there was toward the end of 1998—filming can come to a near standstill.

Shooting can be seasonal, and if there is a flood or disaster, it can halt shooting and with it paychecks. "The business is a gamble," he says, "and you have to be a bit of a gambler to be in it. It's not Las Vegas, but sometimes it feels like it. Ideally, I would like to have a diversified management and production company. Everything I have done has led up to it."

Tisha Fein—who has been a producer as well as the premiere talent coordinator in the business—talks about another kind of pressure. She has been responsible for the talent on virtually every major awards show with the exception of the Academy Awards. One major problem—no shows, or someone who shows up and is too ill to go on stage.

"You can't be faint-hearted as a talent coordinator," she says. "On one recent *Grammy Awards*, Pavoratti could not sing—and we did not find out until that night. You have to remember that these shows are rehearsed, no one is winging it. My job was to get someone to do exactly that." Ms. Fein did: She convinced Aretha Franklin to substitute.

Performers that have to be replaced are one problem, but there are other difficulties as well. Ms. Fein has been involved in shows that have been nominated for Emmys, the Image Awards, and Cable Ace. With that kind of track record, she is constantly in demand.

"Frankly, there are too many shows now, and some are not that good. If you get involved with one that is a stiff, you not only create a great many hard feelings among the artists you booked, but they lose confidence in you. That can hurt down the line. Anyone in—or going into this business—should be careful. Look carefully at what shows you bring talent to because it will impact you throughout your career."

Tony Selznick, the agent who represents choreographers, has run into the same kind of saturation situation that Ms. Fein has seen. Only Selznick's is in the dance area. In the old days of choreography, Bob Fosse and Jerome Robbins were considered the geniuses of the profession. They set the standard. Today, however, Selznick sees the entire dance profession over-crowded with people who are not "truly dancers." It all started with "hip hop," and those who were involved in that craze, got into dance. "It reminds me of when roller skating became the big fad," says Selznick. "We were deluged by roller skaters who said they were dancers. Now we see a lot of people coming out of music videos and saying they are dancers."

One thing appears clear from Selznick's assessment, there are not only a good many untrained dancers and choreographers in the business, but there now appears to be both a classically trained core of dancers versus a hip hop or music video entourage.

A second pitfall that all choreographers (as well as agents) have to wrestle with are credits. Often, the choreographers are not given credit even when they are deeply involved in the production. A good example, says Selznick, is *My Best Friend's Wedding*. The choreographer who did the wedding scene and created the opening title was not listed when the film came out. Why? Most likely, says Selznick, it is because the choreography was not taken seriously. Until it is, agents are going to be wrestling with credits as well as the stature of the profession.

Choreographers are not the only entertainment professionals in the midst of change. Song pluggers or publishing representatives have found themselves in a business that has changed almost as much as dance. In days gone by, most of the songs that were given to artists to record belonged (or were written) by someone else. But, music—and the artists—have changed. Most top-selling singers/performers are writing their own songs, and many publish them as well. For instance, the Beatles penned most of their songs and published them in their own publishing company. Thus, publishing representatives trying to get the foursome to record songs that were not written by the Beatles ran into a stone wall.

NEW PUBLISHING TREND

Artists, particularly those in the rock category, are all doing the same thing. Occasionally, they will take a tune from an old line publishing catalog, but for the most part they are writing and publishing their own. That has cut into many of the catalogs that contain songs penned by songwriters of the last 50 years. Still, Lowy sees no problem, save one, with this trend.

"Their catalogs are mainly administered by attorneys who do not understand the value of exploiting a publishing catalog. Yet, the amount of money they could be generating from the catalogs is enormous. Whereas an artist used to collect two cents for a record (for publishing) now it is seven. That is an enormous difference."

Making up for the lack of publishing royalties that were generated, are new forms and sources of publishing income. Cable and home video have added significant funds to publishing companies, and sheet music continues to sell well. But, what was once a prime source of income—contemporary hit records—is rapidly fading and impacting the business.

Publishing houses created by contemporary artists are not the only pitfall in the business. Technology is on the verge of entering the industry that could download music and bypass the purchase of records. Record companies are suing the manufacturer to stop the sale of the $200 (at retail) gadget that will enable consumers to ignore the traditional channels of record (and publishing) revenue.

Publishing is not the only enterprise that is being threatened from outside sources. Special assignment editor Richard Alvarez sees his profession being buffeted from several forces. A reduction in news staffing is being made possible by the growing number of all-news, all-entertainment channels and outlets. The CBS affiliate in Los Angeles, for instance, has an Orange County bureau. Orange County, which is about 35 miles from downtown Los Angeles, is now being served by Orange County News (OCN). OCN is a profitmaking news service that provides CBS, and other television stations throughout the area, with news stories as well as film. Thus, CBS and others no longer have a need for an Orange County bureau.

CNN MAKING INROADS

Alvarez says the CBS station also gets a feed from Cable News Network (CNN), which eliminates the need for reporters in many other areas. Alvarez says the "business is dying. The craft will continue, but with technology and all the other outlets providing news, a television station or newspaper will be able to put together a story in a half hour or less." Although Alvarez sees this as bad news for many in his position, there is a bright side. As these cable and other outlets gear up, they are going to need reporters and editors. Thus, although the role of an editor with CBS may be diminished, it could be enhanced at CNN or through bureaus like OCN.

Don Graham sees outside forces impacting the record promotion business, as well. With the growing number of formats (everything from adult contemporary, country, to rock), the job of the promotion man is going to be more difficult as they have a narrower niche through which they can promote records. Promotion men are going to have to find those niches and carefully define them and the audiences that are listening. It is going to take more time and manpower, but the change—and niche marketing—has already hit the business.

Although niche marketing has not impacted commercials, there is a definite outside influence that is impacting the business. Whereas commercial announcers used to be able to shout and scream with little problem, the need for sincerity and believability has had an effect on how a spot should be delivered. "Psychology," says Casey Kasem, "plays a big part in the commercial. Sincerity will come through if you have it, but if you do not, the audience is going to know it. And the commercial is going to come out negatively. For all potential (and current) announcers, audiences are sophisticated today, and they recognize what's behind a spot. Is it sincerity or the need to generate money? If they perceive the latter, the spot will not fly. More than ever, commercial announcers have to watch—and feel—sincere about the message they are delivering."

Many of the pitfalls that are sweeping through the industry, and the changes that are impacting it, are rapidly becoming responsible for the future direction (and job descriptions) of those behind-the-scenes entertainment industry workers. Some of the occupations show enormous growth and potential. Take Brick Price and his miniature set designs. "Fifteen years ago, we were told we would only have two or three productive years. That miniatures and special effects would not be that much in demand. Yet, every year our workload has increased and with the films currently on the drawing board, special effects, animation, and set design are going to be bigger than ever."

What's Next in Music

Music publishing has a bright future, too. "It's getting (song catalogs) more valuable every day," says Lowy, "because of the new uses of music. Everything from cable to increased foreign rights. Looming on the horizon, however, is probably the biggest boom for the industry. Right now, we have CDs, but every six or seven years, a new configuration comes along, and all the catalog songs are recut. Just as the 78 RPM went to 45s and 33⅓s, and eventually to cassettes and CDs. The question is what's next? Whatever it is will be a bonanza for the industry."

Rivaling the boom times that Lowy sees is what's happening in the agency field. Tony Selznick sees a number of trends that are not only going to impact choreographers, but they also have the potential to influence the way the entire industry is doing business.

Selznick sees specialization as a wave that is already hitting agencies. Whereas many agencies represent a variety of different artists, Selznick sees that changing in several ways. First, the emergence of boutique agencies will create opportunities for many people who want to break into the business. Much as Selznick's firm represents only choreographers, he sees the same trend sweeping throughout the entire agency business.

"Where would you go?" he asks, "to an agency that specialized in what you do, or to a generalist that handled you and a hundred other artists in different fields? I think most artists would choose the specialist. For one thing, they would feel right at home with their peers, who would also be in the same agency."

Selznick believes there is another force behind this movement. "Most of these boutique operations will be run by people in the business. That is, an agency for choreographers run by a choreographer; an agency for animators run by an animator, and so on. You could even see people with tatoos being represented by tatoo artists. It's doing business with people in your own field. There will be a much higher comfort level for both the artist and the agent."

MTV CHANGED IT ALL

Much of this change Selznick credits to MTV. "They changed everything. They changed the way commercials are being done. Now, you see it is not unusual to have unique characters in ads. Someone with a tatoo or a guy with an earring. A few years back, that would never have gone, but MTV made it palatable."

Selznick sees one other significant change. The movement of agencies into management and production. "It's only natural. The agency has access to the talent, and this has been happening for several years. The bigger agencies first moved into management, then production. But, this won't happen without some court decisions. For instance, as of this writing, one well-known performer was suing his agency because they represent him and his television show. He is negotiating with his own agency. That's going to keep the agency business in flux, for now, but in the long run I think you will see them into production, too."

Casting director Nancy McCook agrees with Selznick in his assessment of the role MTV is playing today. "Credit Calvin Klein with some of the changes. It started with Obsession and it has gone to the point where you find that street people are almost acceptable in commercials. People who are offbeat are in. You can give some of the credit to motion pictures.

"Usually, you find commercial fads running about 18 months behind whatever popular movie was released. Awhile ago, they wanted Tom Hanks for every commercial, then Tom Cruise, Brad Pitt, and Matt Damon. Movies start it but MTV brings it along. Watch the motion pictures for something that really hits, and you will be able to pick the next trend."

Kasem sees voice-overs growing, primarily because of the increased number of radio and television stations, plus the ongoing popularity of cartoon shows, which provide significant business for voice-over specialists.

Despite the commercial demand for Tom Hanks and others, Epstein sees a slacking off on the part of consumers for many of the well-known news and entertainment personalities you see nightly. "I think the days of the high-paid anchor people are over." Epstein could be right. The news media, in particular, has been taking heavy criticism for becoming more important than the news it carries. To add fuel to the thought, network television has been losing audience, and that could be the signal of lower salaries for lower ratings.

FUTURE NEWS TO BE CANNED?

More news in the future will be canned. That is, there will be less newspeople around to cover stories and, consequently, the high-paid anchors and news personnel may become a thing of the past.

There may be differences of opinion as to the future of newscasters and other journalists, but there is solid agreement as to the outlook on the web. Erick Finke—and others agree—that this year there are 100 million documents on the web. In four years, there will be 400 million. Website design firms are growing faster than almost any other business segment of the economy. Finke sees the growth continuing and the future of those dealing with websites among the brightest of any in the entertainment field.

USC's Dean, Rick Jewell, put another twist on the future with the thought that "we are definitely into a new media, an interactive one. None of us can really tell the impact of games in this interactive era, but it could be significant and create an entirely new opportunity in entertainment."

Perhaps producer/director Chuck Bowman summed it up best with this apt analysis of the business. "The most important thing is that this is not a cookie cutter business. We are not providing work for accountants and attorneys. This is truly a business with enormous opportunity—for everyone. You can go where you want . . . and that, truly, is one of the most exciting things about entertainment."

CHAPTER SIX

Inside Tips and a Look Behind the Scenes

In this chapter you will find 32 different entertainment industry occupations, plus hints and tips on how to break into each one. Earning potential, where to launch a career, and how high you can go in the industry through these positions is also detailed in this special section.

PERSONAL ASSISTANT

Tips:	Local television stations and shows, cable stations, radio outlets.
Potential:	Move to associate producer, newsroom, virtually any area.
Bottom Line:	Pay isn't much, around mid-20's but it is a stepping stone.

(Continued)

(*Continued*)

Best Markets: Almost every market has stations to hit. Even management companies have potential.

Drawbacks: Long, irregular hours, poor pay.

Success Stories: Nearly everyone. At least half of the people in this book once had this job title.

INTERN

Tips: Any station, radio or television. In addition, studios, talent agencies, personal managers, and almost anyone in business. Try organizations such as NARAS (National Association of Recording Arts and Sciences) and even Academy of Motion Picture Arts & Sciences. Don't forget agencies, management companies, and cable companies. (See Chapters 4 & 5 for tips.)

Potential: To the top. Almost everyone in this book started as an intern. Great for contacts and learning.

Bottom Line: Bleak. Pay is minimal or non-existent.

Best Markets: Anywhere. If you can't find an intern post, you're not using the right sales approach.

Drawbacks: Long hours, low pay. You have to be on the stick and don't let grass grow under your feet. Take advantage of every opportunity and opening.

Success Stories: One of the best is Chuck Bowman who started as an NBC page and moved up to producing and directing chores; also won an Emmy along the way.

Associate Producer

Tips:	Once again, local media ranging from cable and TV to radio.
Potential:	Once you make it to this level, you're ready for segment post or above.
Bottom Line:	Better than others, can go up to $70,000. More important, a door opener to higher earnings and better positions.
Best Markets:	Locally you should do well. Does not really need LA or NY trip.
Drawbacks:	Just a notch above personal assistant. Duties just as demanding, although many APs are able to move over into talent and booking area.
Success Stories:	Michelle Baxter, John Olds, who moved to exec producer.

Segment Producer

Tips:	Need network or local station that has affiliate, or strong local show. This position may also apply to radio, however, the compensation will not be as great.
Potential:	This sets you up for producer or executive producer post.
Bottom Line:	Decent wage, approaching the six-figure mark. Certainly is the background needed for upward mobility. Means you have had first-hand experience at putting together a show.

(Continued)

(Continued)

Best Markets: Once again, virtually every market—aside from those that are extremely small—will use these people to set up shows. The bigger the market, the better you are equipped to take on major projects.

Success Stories: Bill Royce has done this for the *Jay Leno Show* as well as others. He's one of the most in-demand.

FIELD PRODUCER

Tips: This requires a station that has the capability to send crews out into the field to cover a story. While many local channels have this capability, you will be more likely to find this capability with network affiliates (television and radio). A show such as *Entertainment Tonight* utilizes them, as does most of the other gossip or entertainment oriented shows.

Potential: Great. If someone has shown the confidence in your ability to let you be responsible in the field, then you are usually considered a competent executive. This one has the ability to go all the way up the line.

Bottom Line: This is another one of those positions with excellent salary potential. It depends on the market and the show. Obviously, a major show in a large market is going to pay more than one in a small rural area. But training as a field producer opens the doors for anything. It shows responsibility and the ability to work without direct supervision.

Best Markets:	Larger markets have more opportunity. Does not have to be Los Angeles or New York, but the potential for high income and advancement would be more likely in those cities. Don't forget the Chicago, Philadelphia, and other large metropolitan areas. They use field personnel as much as anyone, however, they do not have the entertainment emphasis or personnel that are found in LA and NY.
Success Stories:	Andy Epstein has been outstanding in this area and his work with Hard Copy has become a standard in the industry.

TALENT COORDINATOR

Tips:	Every talk radio and television show has to have someone book the talent. Good ones— that is—those who can deal with talent without losing their cool are in-demand.
Potential:	Tisha Fein took her skills in this area and today she is one of the most in-demand talent coordinators in the country. She has no trouble dealing with celebrities, which has helped enormously.
Bottom Line:	Definitely one of those six-figure potentials.
Best Markets:	Hollywood, LA, and Nashville are where the big dollars are, but there are many other top 20 markets (i.e., Oprah in Chicago) that rely on talent coordinators. Local markets have need too, although the coordinator in a small market is probably doing double (or triple) duty, and handling a number of other chores.

(Continued)

(*Continued*)

Success Stories: None better than Tisha Fein. Has been involved in Grammy, inaugural for the president, Ford Theater shows for the president, the John Lennon tribute, and dozens of others. She was nominated for Grammy, Image Award, and Cable Ace award. Considered number one in the business.

PUBLICITY REPRESENTATIVE

Tips: If you have writing talent, you can go almost anywhere and get a position as a publicist. Many PR people start as interns with either an advertising agency, PR firm, or both. If you start at the agencies, try volunteering for a nonprofit (locally) to show you can do the job. Another option is to go straight to the management company that handles a performer, and tell them you would like to work (at no cost) because you are in the process of learning the entertainment and PR business.

Potential: The sky is the limit. Many PR people go on to become anything from producers and dirrectors to personal managers.

Bottom Line: An easy six-figure income, especially with entertainment industry clients.

Best Markets: Realistically, PR can be practiced in any city—large or small—but there are not too many cities that have entertainment industry clients unless you are talking about New

York, Los Angeles, Nashville, or Chicago. It is possible to handle an entertainer and be in a market that does not have a dearth of entertainment-oriented shows and/or productions. But, there is little likelihood of a personality living in New York and hiring a PR rep in Des Moines. Anyone looking to make this a career should count on moving to a major market area.

Drawbacks: The media is one. Today, it is difficult to communicate with them, and PR people need to talk to media because they are the people who can "buy" the story that is being pitched and provide the exposure. Voice mail and other obstacles to communication make this a tough job. But, for the aggressive PR person, this can be a great opportunity that financially has enormous rewards.

Success Stories: Craig Miller started this way as did Tisha Fein who became one of the leading talent coordinators in the business by first tackling the PR field where she made—and cemented—numerous relationships. Hollywood and New York are loaded with entertainment PR firms that are enormously successful. Some have grown so powerful that they can even dictate the terms (for a celebrity interview) to the media. PR is a definite entre to the entertainment field.

(Continued)

(Continued)

COORDINATING PRODUCER

Tips:	Almost any major city that has live shows emanating from it. You won't latch on as a coordinating producer to start, but there is a definite chance you can land a job as an intern, runner, and so on for one of the shows. It takes time, but Tisha Fein and others proved it could be done.
Potential:	This opens the door to any major production position. The key is the relationships you can develop with everyone from the show's director to the guests and sponsors. It brings you in contact with all the key players— everyone ranging from talent and sponsors to the other production people who are behind the scenes.
Bottom Line:	As is the case with many other positions that involve live television or a key role behind the scenes, this spot can easily provide someone with a six-figure income.
Best Markets:	Where do you go? To those markets that have (1) live shows that require a coordinating producer and (2) those markets that have the performers. This sounds like Hollywood, New York, or Nashville, but remember there are many markets in the rest of the country that have local artists and variety or other type shows. Measure the market objectively. Does it have the potential?
Drawbacks:	Being in a market that does not have the production capability.

Success Stories: Once again, Tisha Fein. She went from coordinating producer to Grammy winner.

TELEVISION DIRECTOR

Tips: At the bottom of the ladder. Go for internship, production assistant, or any other position that you can land at a television station. Try shooting at the local stations first. If you strike out, go for cable. They are always in need of production help, and will almost always go out of their way to give someone local an internship or (nonpaying) production-oriented job. Be prepared to start at the bottom.

Potential: From television to motion pictures. One is just a step above the other and with TV experience, motion pictures are entirely possible.

Bottom Line: No limit.

Best Markets: It does not matter. You can get started in any market at any station that lets you latch on. Directing shows at the local level can happen much quicker than trying to direct shows in a major area like Los Angeles, New York, Nashville, Chicago, and so on.

Drawbacks: It will not happen overnight. Becoming a director takes time and patience. As Bowman says, "you will not become the captain of the ship overnight." And, while you are working your way up the ladder, the compensation will not be especially high.

(Continued)

(*Continued*)

Success Stories: Bowman is an excellent example of someone who started at the bottom of the ladder (first in Los Angeles, then to the Midwest) and went from menial tasks to co-executive producer, executive producer to director. Bowman says anyone can do it.

CO-EXECUTIVE PRODUCER

Tips: Follow the same path as the director.

Potential: Director is obviously in the offing, along with producer.

Bottom Line: No question, the six-figure incomes are here.

Best Markets: Almost any, although—once again—the markets that are associated with film and television studios would be the best. But there is nothing wrong with someone cutting their teeth in a smaller market, the midwest or a city that is not usually associated with celebrities and entertainment.

Drawbacks: It takes time and patience, and if you are in a smaller market, it will take even more time.

Success Stories: Bowman did it, just check the preceeding entry.

EXECUTIVE PRODUCER

Tips: If you do not have a background in this occupation, you should be starting at ground zero. That is, work as a messenger, intern, assistant producer, page or whatever. This advice may seem redundant, but remember more than 90 percent of those who have made it in the industry started this way.

Potential: No limit.

Bottom Line: Six figures.

Best Markets: Any. But this takes working up the ladder and experience at a variety of other entertainment posts on the way up. When it comes time to establishing yourself, Hollywood or New York should definitely be considered.

Drawbacks: Takes a long time. There is no degree or class you can take to speed up the process. It also requires someone who has ability in a number of areas. Executive producers, like producers, should have the ability to look at the bottom line as well as the lines in the script. It is a difficult, demanding all-around job. The theory is that with the rising costs of features, the producer will—one day— possibly take over the exec's position and be saddled with the duties as well.

Success Stories: None greater than Erica Huggins, executive producer of the film *What Dreams May Come*. Huggins started as an assistant editor and came up quickly. At 35 years of age, she is considered one of Hollywood's bright, up- and-coming young talents.

                                                    (*Continued*)

(Continued)

SCREENPLAY WRITER

Tips:	Hollywood is where it is happening, although there are other markets that produce their own plays and motion pictures for television or the screen. Peter Lefcourt discovered that although New York was a great place, if he wanted to sell a script, he had to be where most of the films are made and the studios are located, Los Angeles. This is where the agents are, as well.
Potential:	Writers can move to directing—especially on television. They can also move to virtually any other behind-the-scenes position they want.
Bottom Line:	This varies with the activity of the writer. Scripts pay well—around $20,000 for an hour-long episode, but the writer has to be productive and have the connections. For those that do, six-figure incomes are real possibilities.
Best Markets:	You can start anywhere, but unless you have a powerful agent in Hollywood who does not require your presence, you need to be on the Coast. Additionally, a Coast location is required for another reason—you have to find an agent for representation.
Drawbacks:	Everyone is writing, from Marsha Clark to Tom Clancy. The glut of writers (8,500 writers today, an increase in Hollywood of nearly 7,000 during the past few years), makes it

tough but it can be done. Ask Clancy and Stephen King.

Success Stories: Lefcourt, certainly, is one. His initial contract went down the sewer when the studio heads rolled. But, he kept pushing and now things are beginning to click for the East Coast writer. Behind him he already has one Emmy, and the fact he was 3,000 miles from Hollywood when his first film script sold, is evidence that success can be achieved by an unknown—regardless of where they live.

COMMERCIAL ANNOUNCER (VOICE OVER)

Tips: Practice in a studio or at home first. Read short stories and get the cadence down. See how others do it. See if you can put a new (and better) emphasis on a commercial spot you hear. You need an agent, and for that a cassette tape. Before submitting it, rehearse and listen. You do not have to do 30 commercials—one good one will do.

Potential: Casey Kasem turned his success into numerous acting roles as well as a promising career. Kasem could have gone on to do a number of things—everything from producing to full-time acting, but he has chosen to concentrate most of his time on voice overs.

Bottom Line: The income level can be in the seven-figure range.

(Continued)

(*Continued*)

Best Markets:	Wherver commercials are happening, and where you will find the agents. Most commercial announcers are provided work by advertising agencies, and most of them are in New York. But, that does not mean other markets are not good. You can start out by doing voice overs for local cable or radio stations. Many will permit you to use their tape facilities in order to practice and improve. Ultimately, you need an agent and a location in a major market (usually Los Angeles or New York) to hit it big.
Drawbacks:	Finding an agent. Although most are willing to listen to a tape, you have to remember they already have clients, many established. It is tough getting someone to listen to a "rookie" when they already have a polished star in the stable. That's why it is important that your tape be the best possible production. It should show you being creative. Remember, in order to get you a job, the agent has to ignore another one of their voice-over announcers. You have to give him good reason to do that.
Success Stories:	There is none greater than Kasem. He had given up all hope of making commercials a career, because an agent disliked his voice. It was only through the urging of a friend that he ultimately got an agent and the rest, as they say, is history.

DISK JOCKEY

Tips:	Anywhere. Every city with a radio station, regardless of size, has a need. Everything from college radio stations to local FM and AM outlets. There are dozens of places to practice and break in.
Potential:	Commercial announcing is a definite possibility, as evidenced by Kasem. Plus, you make contacts in this job that can open doors for other key behind-the-scenes opportunities. Kasem, for instance, built an excellent (but small) acting career thanks to his ability and the people he met initially as a disk jockey.
Bottom Line:	Not everyone is going to be a Casey Kasem, but a well-established disk jockey can easily earn an income in the six-figure range.
Best Markets:	Once again, any. The one difference being that the bigger market usually is going to pay the higher wage. But, it is advisable for anyone seeking this career to hone their skills first—and there is no better place to do that than in a smaller market.
Drawbacks:	You have to have the right voice and you need training. Listen to the radio to get a good handle on what disk jockeys and commercial announcers are listening to. It will be difficult to get played and placed. There is an abundance of good, professional announcers in most of the major cities, but that should not be construed as the death knell. There is opportunity, even if the competition is all over.

(Continued)

(Continued)

Success Stories: Once again, look at Kasem. Another success is Robert Brown, who went from being a classical actor doing Shakespeare to the voice behind Polaroid and Porsche. Brown rose rapidly for several reasons. First, of course, is his voice, but almost as important is his attitude toward commercials and the copy. He does not just read copy, he tries to see what the advertiser (client) is trying to get across. Then he works on it so there is an emphasis on that point. He also endears himself to agencies by adopting a rule— "Don't criticize the copy or you become tense." Don't forget one other thing— "Commercials are a business."

SPECIAL VISUAL EFFECTS

Tips: Hollywood. That's where most special effects studios and enterprises can be found. Learn it from the inside out. As is the case with many other crafts, this one has to be absorbed with you starting out as a production assistant or something similar. Visual effects have become complex, and it requires on-the-job training. Because the craft is so skilled, many visual effects companies are willing to take in a trainee or intern to learn.

Potential: From visual effects you can go into cinematography or a variety of related occupations.

Bottom Line: Brick Price, who has won numerous awards including an Emmy for *Star Trek* and an Oscar for being part of the team for *The Abyss*, says it varies depending upon the schedule in Hollywood. But, as this specialized area gets more notoriety, it's revenue stream could be upped significantly.

Best Markets: Hollywood, where the filmmakers are.

Drawbacks: Price's company is the only one capable of doing specialized cinematography special effects. Thus, the initial opportunities are limited, however, that may change as more visual effects people begin to see the success that Price has had with film. He could be the initiator of an entirely new trend.

PHOTO JOURNALIST

Tips: Stick a pin in a map, and you have a location for anyone who wants to get into the photo journalist business. The opportunities are endless, and prospective photographers can shoot for everyone ranging from nonprofits to local television and newspapers. Getting started is not difficult because most stations have an intern program and are glad to pay a minimal fee for a photo journalist. Wherever you go and shoot, make sure you have a "demo" tape available for showing to stations and others.

(Continued)

(*Continued*)

Potential:	Photo journalists—that is, the good ones—develop an excellent eye that enables them to fit in everywhere from the editing room to the editor's chair. Good photo journalists become excellent story tellers (via film) and if they can tell a good story there is no limit to how high they can go in the entertainment field.
Bottom Line:	Although the base salary for most photo journalists is not in the six-figure range, they have the potential to earn that amount by selling film and stills to studios as freelancers.
Best Markets:	Every market can use a photo journalist. Each television outlet has needs, but the highest paying cities are those with massive audiences and intense competition. That's where the money—and demand usually are.
Drawbacks:	The competition. Everyone wants to shoot film.
Success Stories:	Les Rose stands out. He landed a job with one of the most prestigious stations in the country, and he was 3,000 miles away when he did it. Since then, Rose has turned into a five-time Emmy winner. He might never have got there if an editor had not agreed to interview Rose for a job after the aggressive journalist called him and offered—at his own expense—to fly out for the job interview.

PUBLISHER'S REPRESENTATIVE OR "SONG PLUGGER"

Tips: Try the local record distributor and see if
                     you can get a position as a local radio
                     promotion person. That brings you in
                     contact with the people in both the music
                     and radio business; the key people you
                     need to meet in order to break into the
                     business. If you are in a major market, there
                     is an opportunity to catch on with a
                     publishing company that may need a
                     "plugger' or a "trainee."

Potential: Jay Lowy, a long-time publisher's
                     representative, became president of the
                     National Academy of Recording Arts &
                     Sciences (NARAS).

Bottom Line: Top publisher's reps are responsible for
                     millions of dollars of income, and they are
                     well compensated. Earnings in the business
                     in the six-figure range are entirely possible.

Best Markets: Where there are labels and artists. In that
                     environment, there will almost always be
                     publishing companies and opportunity.

Drawbacks: One phase of the business—artists that
                     record songs from publishers—is
                     diminishing because more artists are writing
                     their own material. That still leaves a big
                     market.

                                                 (*Continued*)

(Continued)

Success Sories: Jay Lowy, who started as a clerk in a retail record store while he was still in the tenth grade, went on to head one of the best-known music publishing houses in the country, Motown's Jobette Music. His idea to turn the soul catalog into a pop music catalog, turned the company into one of the most profitable in the industry.

"FREE FALL" CINEMATOGRAPHER

Tips: This craft combines two skills—skydiving and photography—and is one of the most unusual in the industry. The combination of those two skills is best utilized in Hollywood, where there is sufficient television and motion picture activity. There is only one person who does both the jump and photography (with three cameras) and that's Tom Sanders of Santa Barbara, California. Try convincing Sanders that he needs an assistant. He's the master at the art, and busy enough to where he probably can use a helper, intern, or assistant. It is one of the most unique careers in the business.

Potential: Film editor and/or cinematographer.

Bottom Line: Sanders earns anywhere from $2,000 to $3,000 per jump. Additionally, he sells stills and video to studios and stations. Video footage goes for about $100 a per second, stills anywhere from $30 to $1,000 per shot.

Best Markets:	Sanders is in Santa Barbara, which is about 100 miles from Hollywood. Not being in Hollywood does not seem to hinder his business because it is such a specialty and so few people can do it. The studios have to come to Sanders.
Drawbacks:	Work is not always stable. He depends upon the studios, and if there is a "dry" period, Sanders suffers.
Success Stories:	Sanders is an amazing story. He was afraid of heights and wound up jumping out of an airplane. From that he got the idea to shoot pictures of first-time parachute jumpers; an idea that has turned into a profitable business. What gives Sanders the edge over other jumpers, is that he shoots three cameras when he is falling: video, film, and still. He was the official photographer who accompanied former President Bush when he parachuted to celebrate his birthday.

(*Continued*)

(*Continued*)

CHOREOGRAPHER'S AGENT

Tips:

There is only one firm (as of this writing) that represents choreographers, and the field is wide open. The home of dancing and choreography is southern California. Although New York certainly has its share, the work availability would be greater in LA because of the abundance of motion pictures and television shows that require the skills. Try knocking on some doors if you have the qualifications. If not, ask about interning for awhile. If that doesn't work, volunteer to run errands. Look how Tony Selznick built his firm—a firm that is beginning to make quite a mark in the business.

Potential:

Producing and directing are not out of the question. Right now, Tony Selznick is contemplating doing exactly that. He has the dancers under his wing and it would be an easy step to get involved in production. Anyone following the same path could do the same thing.

Bottom Line:

When films are being made or television shows are being shot, the sky can be the limit.

Best Markets:

Major markets where there is at least television production, and if there are motion pictures being made, that's a plus.

Drawbacks:	Dancing has an image of being passé. Recent films have not done well and will impact the efforts of any firm that is trying to get into the business. That does not mean this attitude will last.
Success Stories:	Tony Selznick has shown what can be done. The former dancer turned choreographer and agent, has built a thriving, young agency. He has managed to get his clients cast in numerous films and television shows ranging from *Evita* and *Titanic* to *Bird Cage* and music videos.

FIELD PRODUCER

Tips:	These are the people who are reponsible for putting together news and entertainment shows in the field or outside the studio. Good newsroom experience is required. Field producer could come from ranks of existing newsmen. Experience could come from coverage of any local events. It is entirely possible for someone without extensive news experience to break into this area. They would have to work their way up starting in the newsroom.
Potential:	Field producer learns every phase of operation while on location. They can easily go on to become news or entertainment producer.
Bottom Line:	Standard is around $3,000 per week, but many of these contracts do not run the entire 52 weeks.

(Continued)

(*Continued*)

Best Markets: Metro areas that have sufficient camera crews. Chances are smaller markets could not afford to support an ongoing field producing operation as a major metropolitan area could.

Drawbacks: The position may not run the full year. Could be for as little as 13 weeks.

Success Stories: Dual Emmy winner Andy Epstein did this on his way to becoming a news show producer. Along the way he won two Emmys.

SPECIAL ASSIGNMENT EDITOR

Tips: Has to have good news and/or journalistic background. Can start in local newsroom as a runner or messenger. May be able to find a position with an existing news show that covers local entertainment or does exposé work.

Potential: Can go all the way to producer of an entertainment magazine show or something comparable in the business. This is a hot position because every entertainment program (and segment) needs someone in this area to dig out the "top" news stories, whether they be entertainment or not.

Bottom Line: Easily a six-figure and above position.

Best Markets: The larger the market the more able the station will be able to afford a special assignment editor. Smaller markets may have this combined with another news position. In larger markets, could have this specifically for an entertainment show as well as for a news show.

Drawbacks: Most markets—except those bigger ones—
may not be able to afford this position.

Success Stories: Richard Alvarez went from a photo journalist
to one of the top special assignment editors
in the country. His experience as a journalist
was the perfect background for this job. He
went on to earn an Emmy for one of the
most celebrated stories of the year—a
multipart feature (all part of special
assignments) that covered the conditions of
restaurants throughout Los Angeles.

COSTUME DESIGNER

Tips: Can start anywhere, but preferably in a
market where there is filming being done.
Don't forget, this is a position that is in
demand from a number of nonfilm entities
such as the Ice Capades, local stage shows,
and so on. Start as an intern or trainee with a
local theater production group, motion
picture studio, or independent film house.

Potential: This job brings you in contact with everyone
in the entertainment business and it gets
you involved with every segment of
production. Can develop from here to
producer and/or director. Can also lead to
show designs for places such as Las Vegas,
Ice Capades, and so on. One of the best
ways to come up through the ranks and
learn about one of the industry's most
important facets.

(Continued)

(*Continued*)

Bottom Line: Depends upon the reputation. Beginners will not, of course, earn what a veteran designer can command. But well-established designers can easily look at six-figure incomes in today's productions.

Best Markets: Confined to those areas that do filming or motion pictures, however, a show town location is also possible, such as Las Vegas, Atlantic City, or New York.

Drawbacks: Not every market has openings for someone with these qualifications. This is a position that relies heavily on the filming of a motion picture, a television special, or some special shows (i.e., Las Vegas). It may be difficult to find steady work.

Success Stories: Bob Schulenberg learned this field by working at Western Costume in Los Angeles. It enabled him to go on and become a designer for shows outside of Hollywood (Las Vegas) and create a career that eventually led him to New York and the advertising world.

ART DIRECTOR

Tips: Virtually any market has a need for this skill including film, advertising agencies, local stage productions. It is possible to hook on to a company by, once again, going for an internship or something as mundane as a messenger. Many of these companies can utilize part-time help since this is an enterprise that can fluctuate in the amount of assignments it gets.

Potential: Anywhere in the business, from film to stage because you see everything and get involved in most areas of the business through this job.

Bottom Line: Depends upon the type of work that is ultimately done. In motion pictures, higher incomes are definitely possible.

Best Markets: Wide open. Depends on what kind of work you desire. For instance, advertising agencies are more plentiful in New York, film in Los Angeles. But every market would have something, even the smaller, local towns have need. Try the local high school and colleges. They have productions and need art directors. Start as a volunteer.

Drawbacks: Like any business related to entertainment, this position frequently is dependent upon the whims of an advertiser or other client. If they do not like what was presented, they can often pressure the agency to get someone new.

Success Stories: Bob Schulenberg used this background when he filmed *Eating Raoul* and it also provided the knowledge he needed when he went on to animation. It all tied together—animation, art, and so on.

(Continued)

(*Continued*)

ANIMATOR

Tips:	Anywhere, great demand. Animation and motion picture studios cannot seem to get enough of them. Openings for trainees and opportunities for interns should be easy. Studios should have openings both for trainees/interns and experienced. If you have ability, this should be an easy entry, at least as a trainee/intern.
Potential:	They can move into positions ranging from producing to directing.
Bottom Line:	For the good ones there is no limit, especially with the apparent shortage today. Salaries are escalating.
Best Markets:	There's no question, if you want to be in the motion picture end, you need to be where it is happening. This one depends heavily on entertainment centers.
Drawbacks:	The technology is constantly changing as is the public's taste. Do they want traditional animation or something more contemporary? What's here today may be gone tomorrow. Especially if a film hits with one type of animation, you can be guaranteed that producers will be shelving other formats in favor of the hot one. Relatively speaking, this is a hot area with few drawbacks.
Success Stories:	All artistic areas are related. Schulenberg did an animation film (five minutes) for his thesis in college and found that animation

---

and design were tied together. Animation helped him when he became a costume designer, and it played an important role when he was named art director of a major New York agency. Most importantly, when he became an illustrator, his experience with animation played a role in his style as well as the quality of the work he turned out.

PRODUCER

Tips:	Few people start at the top. This position takes knowledge of the craft and building. Usually years in the making, but not always a long-term proposition. Start from the bottom up, although Erica Huggins moved on a fast track when she landed a job as assistant film editor. Through that , she learned the ins and outs of film and production. The producer is usually the "den mother" of production. They keep the budget together, solve the internal squabbles on the set (or stage), and help keep the director focused. A mentor can be a significant aid here.
Potential:	You are at (or certainly near) the top. Possibly a director spot.
Bottom Line:	Unlimited. This is the person with enormous responsibility, and the success or the failure of a production usually relies upon this person's skills.

(Continued)

(*Continued*)

Best Markets: Try any, because every production needs a producer, whether it is radio, television, stage, or film. For film, it is Los Angeles and for stage New York would be in the premiere seat. But, don't forget every major city usually has a substantial amount of stage productions going.

Drawbacks: This job has much responsibility, and sometimes many thankless chores, especially when the producer has to settle arguments on the set, petty differences between actors, and try to keep everyone focused on what they should be doing. While acting as the "nanny," the producer seldom gets support from anyone. They are usually responsible for everything that goes on, though.

Success Stories: Bowman is certainly one, but Huggins is an even more of a "Horatio Alger" story. Huggins says one the prime reasons for her success was having two mentors early in her career. One of Huggins' accomplishments and a testament to her ability, was going from editor to producer. Few in the industry ever do that. Before she was 35 years old, she had produced two movies and was executive producer on another major production that starred Robin Williams. While Huggins success has been in film, Bowman has made his mark in television and has produced episodes of some of the highest rated shows around. He did much work for Stephen J. Cannell, considered one of the two or three prime suppliers of network television series.

FILM EDITOR

Tips:	This is definitely a career that involves Hollywood.
Potential:	Depends where you want to steer your career. Editors can become anything from producers and executive producers to directors. They develop (the good ones) a keen sense of storytelling and "film rhythm," that is, determining how good a film "feels."
Bottom Line:	Big dollars for the good ones.
Best Markets:	Once again, Los Angeles is still the film capital and is where most contacts are made.
Drawbacks:	Hard to make inroads without a mentor. Need to get acquainted with those in the business. Without connections, it is difficult to move upward.
Success Stories:	Erica Huggins' initial entry into the field was as an assistant editor. She credits her rapid progress to a pair of mentors who were influential and took a liking to her. Personality and friendliness is important in the business, especially when someone is starting out.

FILM PROMOTER

Tips:	Internships with promotion firms, studios, and independent film makers. Best cities, of course, are where the films are being made which means, once again, a place such as Los Angeles.

(Continued)

(Continued)

Potential:	Promoters have several advantages. First, they deal with all the key people who are involved in filmmaking, hence they make solid contacts without having to climb the ladder. They also have the ability to watch filmmaking from the inside and absorb what is going on in the different professions. Thus, they have the rare opportunity of being able to evaluate the pros and cons of different positions before they commit to any one of them. Promoters have gone on to become producers, animators, directors— you name it.
Bottom Line:	Good pay for a demanding, creative job. Promoters—that is, those people who develop promotional tie-ins, promotions, and so on for film—need to be imaginative. The industry pays well for that, and six-figure incomes are common.
Best Markets:	Once again, where films are made. Although promoters can get indoctrinated into the business in most markets, because every business, whether it is entertainment oriented or not, needs a promoter.
Drawbacks:	On the outside looking in. You're not really a member of the creative team that put the film, motion picture, and so on together. Thus, the promoter's contribution is often overlooked.
Success Stories:	Craig Miller went from niche promotion (science fiction) to animation and a writer of some of television's best-known and highest rated shows.

DEVELOPER

Tips:

This is not the person who develops film, but rather it is the person(s) who develop series, and ideas. Primarily a creative individual (or group of them). They can come from the ranks of the writers, producers, directors, or any other occupation within the industry, because everyone usually has an "idea" for a series, motion picture, and so on. The trick is developing it and then selling to a company that will provide the financing. Some people may just have an idea, and if the company doing the financing likes it, they may hire someone to develop it more fully. The interesting aspect to a developer is that they do not have to be someone who is high up in the industry. Frequently, they may just be someone who has an idea with little or no experience in the business, but they possess an excellent concept.

Potential:

Good developers are not only creative, but they are salespeople as well. They might, for instance, acquire the rights to a cartoon character and develop a series from there. They might then become the producers of the series and go out and try to get financing for it. They can go on to become executive producers, producers, and directors.

Bottom Line:

Excellent earning potential easily in the seven-figure range if series is successful.

(*Continued*)

(*Continued*)

Best Markets:	Where the action is. If you want to sell a television series (idea) you need to be in Los Angeles or possibly New York. Most stage work is still done in New York.
Drawbacks:	Could be a feast or famine business. You can have a million ideas, but the trick is to sell them. To know what the networks, independents, cable channels will buy. It also takes a long time between conception, development, sale—and income. Additional drawback is that the idea for the show, script, concept, and so on may belong to the developer, however, if someone else is doing the financing, the developer will often lose control of the show. This can create conflicts, especially when it gets to the creative end of the business.
Success Stories:	There are many successful developers around, such as Stephen J. Cannell. Craig Miller, who started as a promoter, got into the development business through his penchant for animated series and script writing. Miller acquired the rights to a cartoon character, developed them, went out to different companies (as producer) seeking the financing. Miller and his coworkers eventually selected BKN, which gave the group the best opportunity to retain control of the show. Miller created and became one of the executive producers.

WEBSITE PRODUCER

Tips:	Website producers are in every market.
Potential:	Can make the Web a career or spinoff into entertainment.
Bottom Line:	Earning potential is unlimited because of the growth of the Internet and the number of companies that are discovering that they need a presence on it.
Best Markets:	Once again, all. Of course, a market with more corporations is going to be better than one without. But the advantage of dealing in this area is that you can be headquartered in one market, and work for a company (freelance) in another.
Drawbacks:	Not many. It's a wide-open market, but if there is a drawback, it is convincing companies that you can do the work. There are hundreds of website producers roaming the streets, and many have "burned" companies, consequently, there is a suspicion of website producers and what they can (or cannot) accomplish.
Success Stories:	Website producers are picking up anywhere from $50,000 and up for design of sites. Erik Finke's firm had the perfect background. They started with local (cable) television and learned what it takes to make something visually attractive enough to generate viewers. Designing a good television show with high ratings involves the same skills as putting together an

(Continued)

(Continued)

Success Stories: attractive, effective website. Finke got involved in the Internet three years ago, and used his local cable television learning experience to provide the foundation for his approach to potential clients. His theory that the Internet and good websites are no more than "interactive storytelling" has helped him build a young, rapidly growing company.

PERSONAL MANAGER

Tips: It takes an astute businessman who is willing to put on another hat and not only handle a client's business affairs, but their emotional problems as well. Business managers could well be the psychologists of the entertainment business.

Potential: Many are going into production because they have access to the clients who are needed to be featured (or starred) in motion pictures, television and the theater. If you managed Tom Cruise or Tom Hanks, you would have the opportunity to become an executive producer or producer of any film in which they starred. Personal managers have clout (that is, if the client listens to them).

Bottom Line: Usually a percentage of the gross of the artist's income. Can be anywhere around 10% to 15% of gross, sometimes more.

Best Markets: Where the action is. You need to be where the people are who need personal managers, and most of those in the entertainment business are concentrated in three markets—New York, Los Angeles, and Nashville.

Drawbacks: Balancing act at times. You have to be able to listen and be empathetic to an artist who has personal problems. The dealings are not always objective and cut and dried. Many times an artist's personal life (and problems) enters into the picture (and deal you are negotiating or hoping for). At the same time, you also have to remain objective because you have to deal with studios, agents, producers, directors, writers, on your artist's behalf. If the artist has a bad break or misses out on a part/assignment, they frequently blame the personal manager. The manager usually gets little credit when something (from a career standpoint) goes right, but all the blame when it goes wrong.

Success Stories: Paul Addis has built a significant stable of successful artists in the music field. He started by working in a music store and meeting both artists and prospective artists who wanted to get into the business. Addis found that he had the sales ability to put together record deals (i.e., Caldera with Capitol) and handle tours, negotiations, publicity, and business dealings. Today, Addis runs Ambitious Entertainment, and

(Continued)

(Continued)

Success Stories: concentrates on managing directors, photographers, and designers, the three occupations he believes are critical to most commercial productions, which his company specializes in producing.

INDEPENDENT CASTING DIRECTOR

Tips: This is an entrepreneurial type position where studios and agencies may come to an independent to help find someone who can fill a specific (usually commercial) role. The independent does not have talent signed to them. Instead they go out and find the talent by approaching other agents who do have talent signed. Try working for a talent agency, commmercial firm in order to get a feel as to how the business works. Some will hire interns. Academy of Television Arts and Sciences has an intern program. William Morris has an agent training program, and most production companies have ground floor opportunities for those wanting to get into the business. This position has few barriers and lots of opportunity.

Potential: Finding and judging talent (if you are good at it) can lead to numerous positions in the industry. The independent can become an agent working for an agency, a producer or executive producer. Being able to find talent and judge it well is a remarkable skill that is needed in the business.

Bottom Line: Independents with excellent judgement are in-demand by agencies and clients who are always looking for commercial talent that the audience can identify with and believe. Finding someone of that ilk is a challenge and for the independent who can consistently come up with the right talent, there is no end of opportunity for earnings.

Best Markets: Most commercials (and talent demand) are in the major metropolitan areas. That, of course, means New York, Los Angeles, and Chicago, but virtually every local community has a need for talent to be featured in commercials.

Drawbacks: Competitive and you have to convince agencies and commercial clients that you can produce the right talent; talent that will help them sell their products.

Success Stories: There aren't many better than Nancy McCook who started as a switchboard operator in a commercial agency and learned the business from there. Nancy went on to handle talent (as an agent) on both coasts and worked with everyone from Herschel Bernardi to Howard Morris.

(Continued)

(Continued)

Commercial Agent

Tips:	Same places as for independent casting director. Big difference is the agent handles the client (talent) whereas the casting director works primarily for the studio, agency, and so on that is searching for the talent. (See independent casting director for ways of breaking into the field.)
Potential:	Equivalent to that of the independent casting director. Years ago, commercials were not considered "career-enhancing" by personalities, however, with the dollars currently being waved in front of them there is little difficulty in getting a personality (with some exceptions) to do a commercial. The good agent not only brings a lot of work to their client (the celebrity) but they also make contacts. Good judgment on an agent's part is one of the requirements for a producer, or executive producer.
Bottom Line:	Good income, especially if you represent well-known personalities who can usually command significant fees for commercial appearances.
Drawbacks:	Handling personalities means that you may be dealing with people who are demanding. You have to not only be selling your clients, but understanding of some of their problems. In other words, the casting agent not only has to dig up business, but in many ways they are acting as a manager, and they

suddenly may find themselves helping the personality (talent) with problems they did not count on handling.

Success Stories: There are hundreds of prosperous agents including Nancy McCook who was one before opting to switch from agent to independent. Either way, she—and many others—have found that making a career out of generating commercial work for entertainers can be extremely rewarding—and profitable.

Index